CREATIVE PATTERN DESIGNING

CREATIVE PATTERN DESIGNING

ANN EVANS

DAVID & CHARLES
Newton Abbot   London   North Pomfret (Vt)

This book is dedicated to my father, Donald J. W. Giddins,
whose love of writing and drawing were absorbed
during long hours working to support our family.
My love and thanks to you and to Mum always.

British Library Cataloguing in Publication Data

Evans, Ann
   Creative pattern designing.
   1. Dressmaking——Pattern design
   I. Title
   646.4'3204   TT520

   ISBN 0-7153-8822-3

Phototypeset by Typesetters (Birmingham) Ltd,
Smethwick, West Midlands
and printed in Great Britain
by Butler & Tanner Ltd, Frome
for David & Charles Publishers plc
Brunel House   Newton Abbot   Devon

Published in the United States of America
by David & Charles Inc
North Pomfret   Vermont 05053   USA

Contents

Introduction

For centuries people have been able to sew their own clothes, but often for one reason or another the finished product is frustratingly wrong for them. The aim of this book is to increase your knowledge of basic pattern making, thus enabling you to create designs that will flatter your own figure and to use individual flare to disguise any imperfections if necessary.

The necessary basic body 'block' is entirely made from direct body measurements. These are applied to a flat pattern and made into a fabric 'toile'. Any alterations are then made until a perfect fit is achieved. From the perfected pattern it will be easy to apply basic designing techniques and to create an endless source of designs.

The cost of equipment for making patterns is very low and of course, making your own clothes can save a small fortune. You will also have the satisfaction of knowing that your outfit is unique.

Equipment
Folder with plain paper
Pencils – medium or fine lead
Felt-tip pens, fine point – one black, one red
Tape measure
Sellotape
Scissors for cutting paper
Flexible curve – 51cm (20in) from art suppliers
White cardboard – 76×51cm (30×20in), two to start with
Ruler
Yard rule
Scales – traced from this book (Chapter 3) glued to stiff cardboard
Paper for patterns – the end of roll from a newspaper printer is fine. (More helpful is 2.4cm (1in) square ruled paper, 76cm (30in) wide)

Abbreviations
B=back
F=front
CB=centre back
CF=centre front
NP=neck point
SP=shoulder point
T=top point (of sleeve)
RS=right side (of fabric)
WS=wrong side (of fabric)

1 Visual effects of design

Creating Illusions

Although it is always necessary to make the basic blocks before actually starting to design, it is a good idea to find out what your ultimate aim will be. By simply using lines in designs it is possible to create an illusion to direct attention to good points on your figure and consequently take attention away from our imperfections. Remember vertical lines lengthen; horizontal lines widen.

Let's take a look at four vertical lines, identical in length:

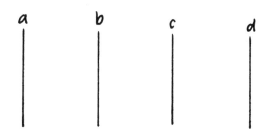

Now look at the same four lines below. (a) has been left as it is. A horizontal line has been drawn across the top of (b). Lines sloping down resembling an arrow have been added to (c) and up, resembling a Y, on (d).

(d) now looks longer than the others and (c) the shortest. (b) gives a wider appearance. These lines can be applied to your designs.

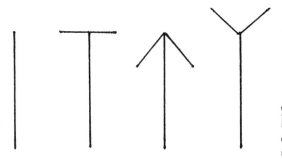

Texture and colour can be used to enhance lines and divert the eye. A short, heavy-busted figure would benefit from the (d) line. If another darker colour or texture giving depth were used in the top section this would minimise the bust size and give height. The 'T' effect of (b) would give width to the shoulder line and minimise a large waist.

Learn to play down faults. If large hips give you a triangular appearance, try wearing a soft lined skirt (slight flare) and at the same time create a top with maybe a flounced collar or unusual sleeves (Fig i overleaf).

Fig i   (left) short with large hips; (right) tall with large hips

Fashion trends are tempting to follow but are not for everyone. Imagine a Twenties-style, low hip-lined, dress on a short person. This would create a rectangular impression cut in half, thus minimising height and adding more width. It would be better to redesign the dress with a basic suitable shape, then add a popular Twenties collar or sleeve (Fig. ii).

Consider your fabric when designing. It would be a waste of time to make an elaborate design in a dense floral pattern as the fabric would consume the lines. Design for your fabric and not vice versa. Try on store clothes to discover which colours, sleeves and necklines are the most flattering for you.

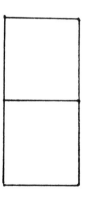

Fig ii

2 Taking measurements

We are going to use the direct measurement method of flat pattern making and for this you will need to obtain an accurate account of your measurements. It is best to wear good underwear and just a T-shirt over for this.

Do NOT allow seam allowances or ease. The seam allowances are not marked on the basic patterns but ease is worked out for you and is roughly 5cm (2in) in the bust, 2.4cm (1in) in the waist and 3.6cm (3in) in the hips. Enlarging and reducing of patterns will be discussed in Chapters 13 and 16.

Bust   Measure around the fullest part, keeping tape measure at same level around back.

Waist   Breath comfortably.

Hips   Take tape over the largest part. Hold tape at hip measure and ease down over thighs. If thigh measurement is more than hips record this.

Back length   From nape of neck to waist.

Front length From shoulder, directly above fullest part of bust, to waist.

Front chest   Usually 10.2cm (4in) below pit of neck, across to arms. This will be where your sleeves will 'sit' so measure to where it will be comfortable.

Across back   Across broadest part, arm to arm.

Sleeve length With bent arm, from top arm to elbow, continue to wrist. (Measuring down shoulder, elbow and wrist bones is most accurate.)

Fig i

Fig ii

Fig iii

Women's Measurements

The following chart gives average measurements used by commercial pattern companies. We can use them for comparisons and if you are thinking of designing on a large scale then a block of each size is helpful. More important, we will use their measurements for 'neck' and 'dart' widths as these are awkward to take from direct body measurements. Use the nearest to your bust size. If you are between sizes, judge by frame, ie a large framed, 94cm (37in) busted person should use the 96.5cm (38in) size, whereas a small framed, 89cm (35in) busted person should use the 86.5cm (34in) size.

Shoulder measurements are worked out from the back block, which is constructed first. 'Length to bust point' can be taken at the same time as 'length over bust point to waist'. The latter should be taken from the shoulder, directly above the fullest part of the bust, to bust centre (see Fig i).

The arm circumference measurements require additional ease to suit each individual. Measuring a comfortable sleeve from a blouse should give you an ideal measurement.

All other measurements should be recorded in exact body measurements. Ease is worked out for you and added to the front blocks.

NB The measurements are given in centimetres with inches in brackets throughout. Fill in your own measurements in the last column.

Bust	76 (30)	81 (32)	86.5(34)	91.5(36)	96.5(38)	101.5(40)	106.7(42)	....
Waist	56 (22)	61 (24)	66 (26)	71 (28)	76 (30)	81 (32)	86.5(34)	....
Hips	84 (33)	89 (35)	94 (37)	99 (39)	104 (41)	109 (43)	114 (45)	....
Nape of neck to waist	37.5(14¾)	38 (15)	38.7(15¼)	39.5(15½)	40 (15¾)	40.7(16)	41.2(16¼)	....
Length over bust point to waist . . . Add 3.2cm(1½in) to back length for commercial								
Length to bust point								
Across chest	34.2(13½)	35.5(14)	37 (14½)	38 (15)	39.5(15½)	40.7(16)	42 (16½)	....
Across back	31.7(12½)	33 (13)	34.2(13½)	35.5(14)	37 (14½)	38 (15)	39.4(15½)	....
Sleeve length	56 (22)	57 (22½)	59.7(23½)	62.2(24½)	65 (25½)	65 (25½)	65.5(25¾)	....
Top arm	....add ease							
Elbow	....add ease							
Wrist	....add ease							
Neck width	5.4(2⅛)	5.7(2¼)	6 (2⅜)	6.3(2½)	6.7(2⅝)	7 (2¾)	7.3(2⅞)	....
Dart width	5.7(2¼)	6.3(2½)	7 (2¾)	7.6(3)	8.3(3¼)	8.9(3½)	9.5(3¾)	....
Shoulder to elbow . . . for dart position of fitted sleeve								
Waist to hipline length								

Taken sideways, from waist to fullest part of seat, this measurement depends a lot on height and body torso length. As a general rule:

157–162cm (5ft 2in–5ft 4in)= 20.3cm (8in)

165–172cm (5ft 5in–5ft 8in) = 22.9cm (9in)

over 175cm (5ft 9in) = 25.4cm (10in)

3 Quarter scales

Trace this quarter scale plus the following quarter-scale blocks onto paper. Paste onto a fairly stiff card and cut out. You will save hours of practice and designing time by using these, compared to full scale and you will save in materials too.

All of the following scales are for a basic 91.5cm (36in) bust size.

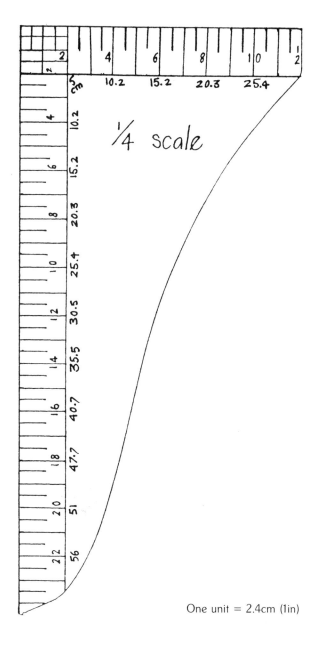

¼ scale

One unit = 2.4cm (1in)

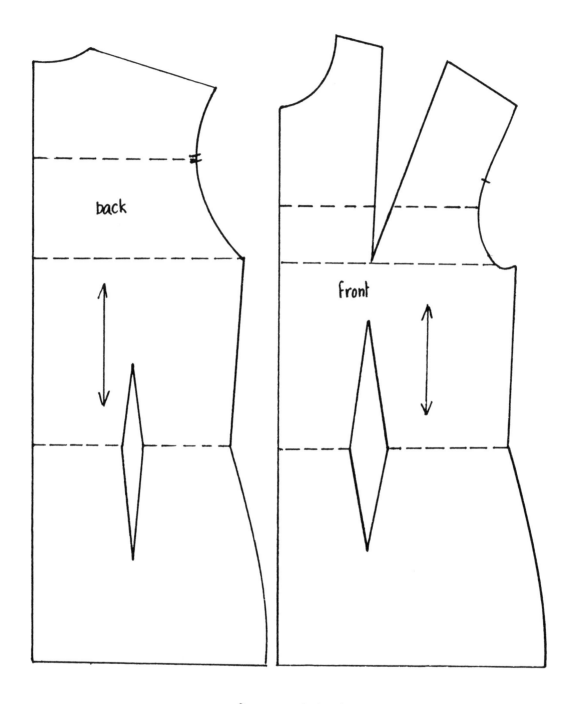

back

Front

front and back
with corrected
shoulder

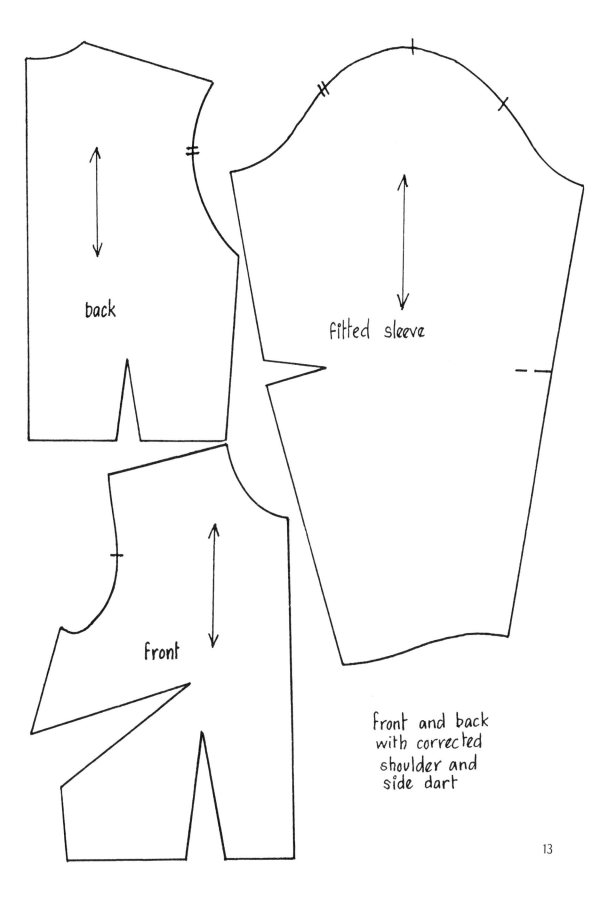

back

fitted sleeve

front

front and back
with corrected
shoulder and
side dart

13

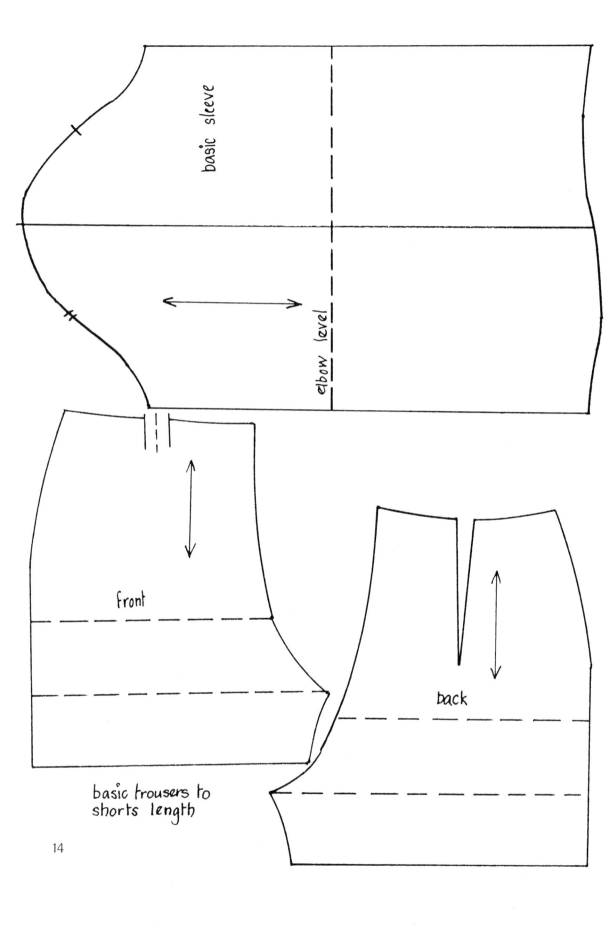

basic sleeve

elbow level

front

back

basic trousers to
shorts length

14

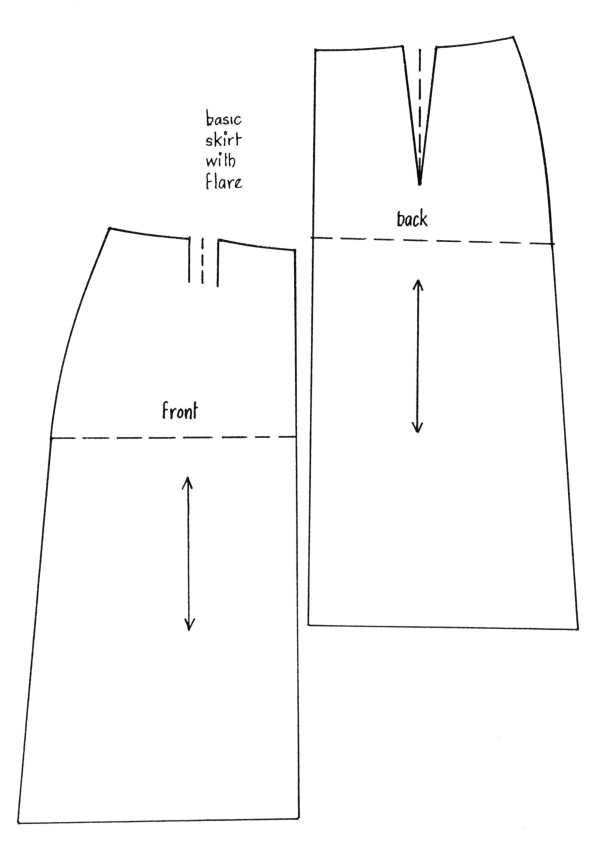

basic
skirt
with
flare

back

front

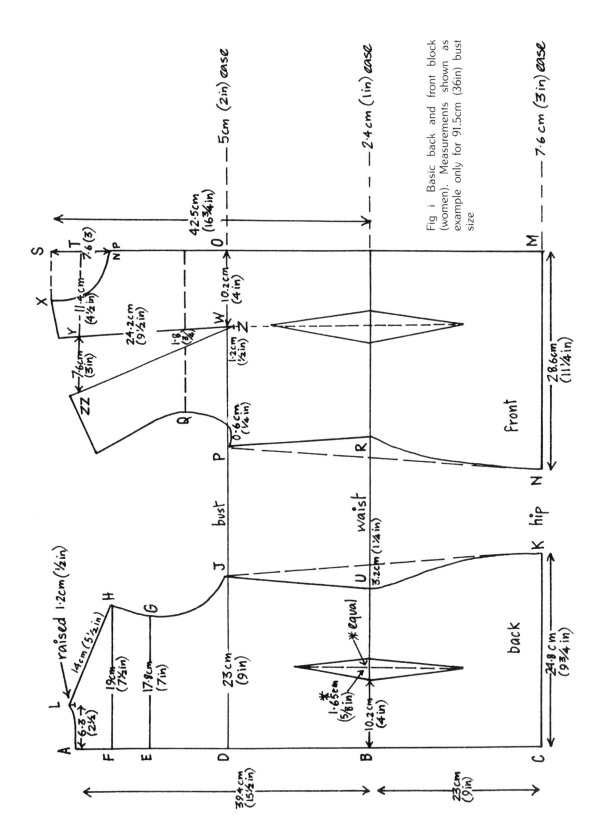

Fig i Basic back and front block (women). Measurements shown as example only for 91.5cm (36in) bust size

4 Basic back and front blocks

Now you are ready to start and make the back and front basic blocks. Use your quarter scale to practise making these blocks which are for a 91.5cm (36in) bust size. Capital letters are used to connect points. The figures in square brackets after each step are for the basic 91.5cm (36in) size.

Back Block

Following Fig i opposite, draw a vertical line to represent the centre-back line on the left of your paper. Start 7.5cm (3in) down from the top of the paper.

1 AB = neck to waist measure at centre back. Draw waist line across. [39.4cm (15½in)]
2 BC = hip line. Draw hip line across. [23cm (9in)]
3 AD = bust level. Draw bust line across. [20.2cm (8in)]
4 AE = 10.2cm (4in), all sizes. From E apply half the across back measure to G. [17.8cm (7in)]
5 AF = 4.5cm (1¾in), all sizes. From F apply the measurement from E to G plus 1.2cm (½in) to H. [19cm (7½in)]
6 DJ = half the across back measure, E to G plus 5cm (2in). [23cm (9in)]
7 CK = a quarter of the hip measure. [24.8cm (9¾in)]
8 Connect J to K.
9 Connect HGJ to form the curved armhole.
10 On line JK, at waist level, mark a point for the waist shaping 3.3cm (1¼in) in to U. Connect these points to J and K to form the side seam, curving over hip. (Look at hip shape for your own block.)
11 AL = neck width. Apply nearest measure to your own from the chart on women's measurements (Chapter 2). Square up 1.2cm (½in) at point L. Connect L to H to form shoulder line. Draw neck curve. [6.3cm (2½in)]
  On the waist line, mark a point midway

between B and U for the back dart position. Draw a central vertical line, 10.2cm (4in) above the waistline and 12.7cm (5in) below. The amount in the dart depends on the fit required but as a guide, take away a quarter of the waist measurement from the surplus, BU, ie BU on the 91.5cm (36in) block measures 21cm (8¼in). Our required waist measure is 71cm (28in) total. ¼ of this is 17.8cm (7in). Take away the difference to reach 3.2cm (1¼in). This is the total dart size. Divide equally each side of central dart line. [1.65cm (⅝in)]

For figures with very small waist measurements it will sometimes be necessary to make two darts. On the other hand, large waisted figures very often end up with no dart at all. Draw in the position however as it can be helpful with princess styles.

Draw the bust, waist and hip lines completely across the page in preparation for the front block. Your quarter-scaled block should measure the same as Fig i.

Front Block

This is perhaps the most complicated part of pattern making so a little more patience is required. However isn't it good to know that once the front block is completed every other will be easier!

1 On the right side of your paper, draw a line to represent the centre front (Fig i). Allow enough room to apply quarter of the hip measure plus 10.2cm (4in).
2 MN on the hip line = ¼ of the hip measure, plus 3.6cm (1½in). [28.5cm (11¼in)]
3 OP on the bust line = bust measure plus 5cm (2in) minus the total back measure from the back block DJ, then halved. [91.5+4.8 = 96.3. 96.3−45.8 = 50.5. 50.5÷2 = 25.2cm. (36+2 = 38. 38−18 = 20. 20÷2 = 10in.)
4 Connect P to N.
5 From waist position on CF line, apply the

17

measure taken from the shoulder, over bust to waist. This is generally 3.2cm (1¼in) longer than the back measure A to B. [42.5cm (16¾in)] Call this point S. Draw a horizontal line from S, about 10.2cm (4in).

6 SX = the neck width (same as A to L on back). On CF line mark a point 7.6cm (3in) below S. Connect X to this, neck point, to form the curved neckline.

7 ST = 3.2cm (1¼in), all sizes. From T mark a point 11.4cm (4½in) across to Y.

8 Bust line OW = 10.2cm (4in). This measurement, between bust points, can be adjusted to the individual figure.

9 Mark a point 1.2cm (½in) below WZ. From Z draw a line to represent the right side of the shoulder dart, through Y and the measure 'length to bust point'. [24.2cm (9½in)]. If the line goes above the line SX, ignore the Z point and measure down from the SX line. This sometimes happens on lower-busted or square-shouldered figures.

10 From Y measure across the dart width (from chart to nearest bust size). [7.6cm (3in)]

11 From Z, or bottom of dart, measure up the exact same measure as the right side, the left side of the dart, calling this ZZ. [24.2cm (9½in)]

12 By cutting down one side of the dart, fold the dart together as if sewing. From point X apply the shoulder length, taken from the back LH, running through the top dart points, ZZ* (Fig ii). Unfold dart. [14cm (5½in)]

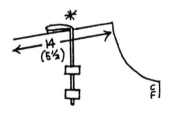

Fig ii

13 From NP on the CF line mark a point 10.2cm (4in) down to represent the chest line. Horizontally apply half the across chest measure plus the amount in the dart at this level, to Q. [38÷2 = 19. 19+1.8 in

dart = 20.8cm (15÷2 = 7½. 7½+¾ in dart = 8¼in)]

14 Draw a line to form the armhole, curving from shoulder through QP, but dropping 0.6cm (¼in) on the bust line to allow for a comfortable fit.

15 On the line PN, at waist level, mark in 3.2cm (1¼in) to R. Draw in side to match back.

16 Make front waist dart by drawing a vertical line 5cm (2in) below Z to 12.7cm (5in) below waist line. The dart width = the difference between a quarter of waist measure, with 2.4cm (1in) ease, and the amount now in the block. [73.6cm (29in)] There is 35.6cm (14in) left in the back 91.5cm (36in) block after its darting. We need 38cm (15in) in the total front. Our block measures 24cm (9½in) from CF to R, thus making a total front measure of 48cm (19in). We need 19cm (7½in) so we must take a 5cm (2in) dart. Mark a point 2.4cm (1in) each side of central line. Connect to top and bottom points to form dart. If you are unsure how to make this dart just mark the central line and you will be able to pin one into the fabric toile you will soon be making.

When you feel confident at constructing the front and back blocks following the 91.5cm

fold

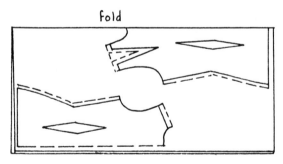

(36in) size in quarter scale, make a quarter-scale block using your own measurements. These will also be useful pasted on card for designing at a later stage.

Next, draw your own block in full scale using 2.4cm (1in) square ruled paper.

The best way to tell if your pattern fits correctly is to make a fabric toile. A toile is a close fitting 'shell' made in fabric. Use a woven fabric, preferably a cotton (an old sheet is fine). Knits will stretch and give a false sense of fit. You will need 1 metre (1yd) of 115cm (45in) wide fabric. Allow more for larger sizes.

Add seam allowance of 1.2cm (½in) to the shoulders, back and side seams. The CF is placed on the fold. The neck and armhole lines remain to help see finished curves.*

Cut out.

Stitch shoulders, side seams and darts. Leave an 46cm (18in) back opening but stitch below. Strengthen neck and armhole edges with stay-stitching using a large machine stitch.

Adjustments that may have to be made

Neck Too High or Armhole Too Tight

1 To amend either of these problems, draw in desired line directly onto toile at fitting (Fig i). Take off toile. Cut away fabric on these new lines.

2 Apply cut away pieces to your paper pattern. Draw around corrected shape. Cut away pattern (Fig ii).

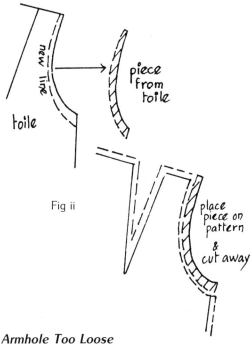

Fig ii

Armhole Too Loose

1 Fold away surplus fabric as a dart. Taper dart to end of shoulder dart (Fig i). Measure from shoulder seam on toile to dart at armhole edge. Measure amount in dart, at armhole (Fig ii).

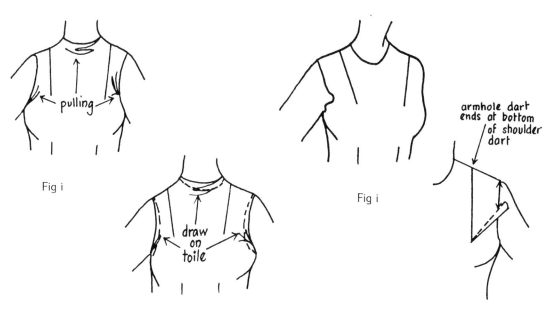

Fig i

Fig i

19

2 Apply these measurements to your pattern. Close out the dart by securing with tape (Fig iii). The shoulder dart will now be wider.

1 Pin out amount puckering like a dart (Fig i).
2 Cut away bodice at waist level (Fig ii).

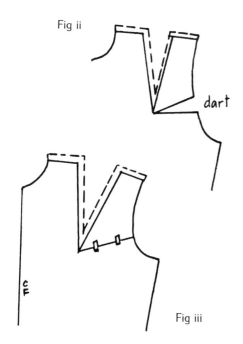

Fig ii

dart

c
F

Fig iii

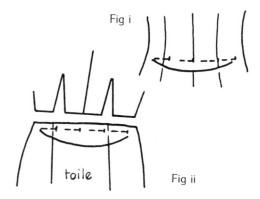

Fig i

toile

Fig ii

3 Measure pinned dart. Apply this measurement to the waist level of skirt. (Line will be curved.) Cut away on curved line (Fig iii).

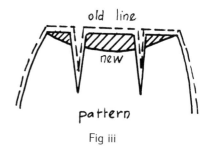

old line

new

pattern

Fig iii

You will now have a smaller armhole, but it will not be necessary to make a dart in garments. Shoulder dart will be larger as it now contains the armhole dart.

Ridge Above Hips Below Waist
(usually caused by a hollow back)

You will need to design garments with a waistline in the back as it is not possible to connect the bodice and skirt again.

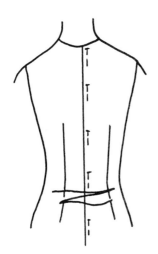

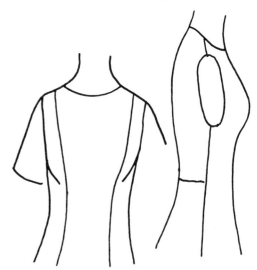

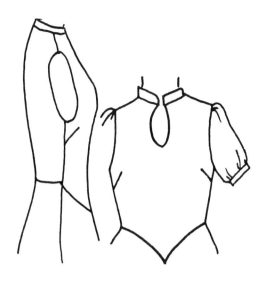

Adjusting Excess Amount in Back Armhole
(when fullness cannot be dispersed into a seam)

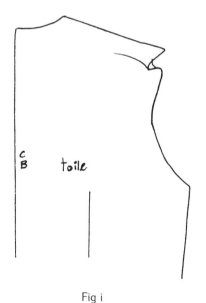

Fig i

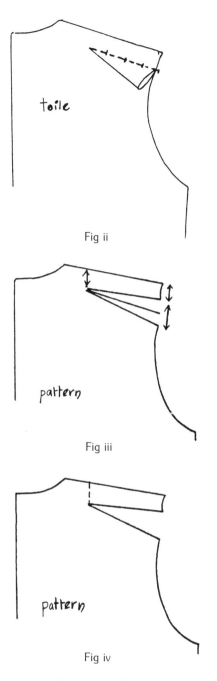

toile

Fig ii

pattern

Fig iii

pattern

Fig iv

Sometimes the back toile puckers into the armhole and ends below the shoulder line when surplus fabric is pinned out (Fig i). In this case the front usually fits smoothly. If the shoulder line is to be adjusted too it may be easier to do that first (see page 22).

1 Pin out surplus into a dart, ending where back is smoothest (Fig ii).
2 On toile take measurements from shoulder to dart, then width of dart. Apply to pattern (Fig iii).
3 Draw a line directly above end of dart into shoulder line (Fig iv).

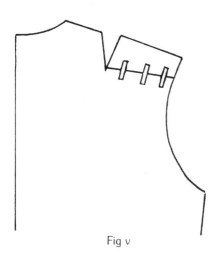

Fig v

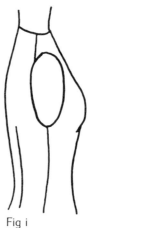

Fig i

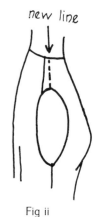

new line

Fig ii

4 Cut down vertical line to end of dart. Close armhole dart, thus opening surplus into a shoulder dart (Fig v).

3 Cut away on new line (Fig iii), usually on the front, and add piece to back (Fig iv).

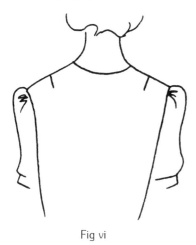

Fig vi

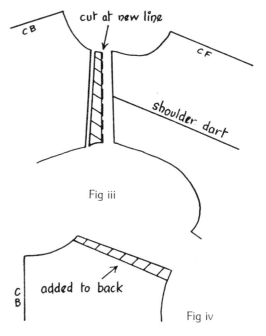

Fig iii

Fig iv

The back shoulder dart is hardly noticed in any design but will always be necessary for a good fit (Fig vi).

Adjusting the Shoulder Line

The shoulder line on the basic block does not run straight along the shoulder. In almost every case it will go towards the back, over the shoulder (Fig i).

1 Try on your toile. Draw in a central shoulder line (Fig ii). Measure and transfer the new line position to your pattern. Folding the shoulder dart together is helpful.
2 Make a note on the neck edge of the piece to be cut away.

Don't forget to ignore seam allowances that were added to make the toile. These will be cut away from the corrected pattern as designs are made without them.

When all adjustments have been made to the pattern, cut away all seam allowances. Trace the patterns and paste onto fairly stiff card. Alternatively, draw around the patterns directly onto the card.

These basic 'blocks' can be made for all the basic patterns and save time in designing.

5 Basic dart positions

The first thing you must consider when designing any top is the position of the dart. The dart is put into the shoulder on the basic blocks for the best possible fit especially across the chest. The shoulder dart can be moved to five basic positions. For practice, take some spare paper and draw around the basic front block to the waist level. You will need five blocks.

The Underarm Dart

1 Draw a line from the bottom of the shoulder dart to the side seam, at position required. Fold out the shoulder dart with pins, as if it were being sewn, or tape lightly together.

2 Cut along new line to bust point (bottom of shoulder dart). The dart will now open and although it seems narrower it is the exact size for you (Fig i).

In the Waist

Follow the instructions for dart 1, but drawing new line into waist area. Waist may be darted by making existing waist dart larger (Fig ii).

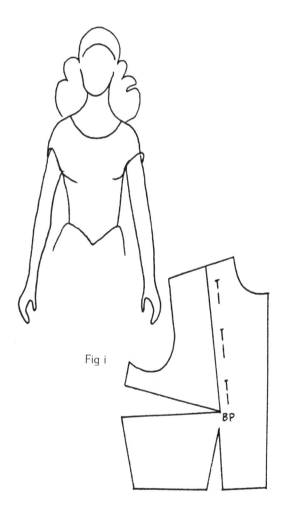

Fig i

BP

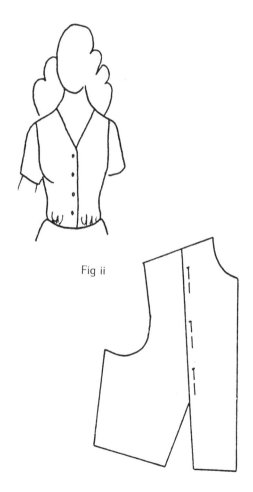

Fig ii

or

Dividing amounts into two small darts (Fig iii). Trace Fig ii, place darts to required position and divide dart size in half.

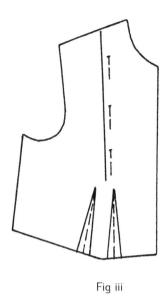

Fig iii

or

Gathering along the waistline (Fig iv). Do not gather just between amount in dart. Spread evenly each side of new dart lines depending on style desired.

Fig iv

On the Shoulder

Follow instructions for dart 1 but draw new dart line to another position on the shoulder. For a comfortable fit and to avoid bulky sewing at neckline, the dart should be no nearer than 2.4cm (1in) to neckline.

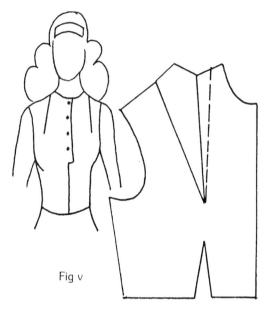

Fig v

In the Neckline

Follow instructions for dart 1 with new line going into neckline. Neckline may be darted but is usually gathered. Gathering lines should start about 2.4–3.6cm (1–1½in) each side of dart line.

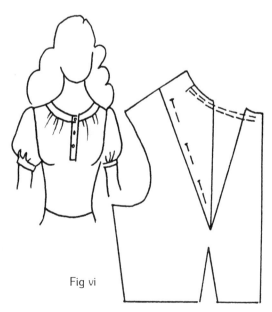

Fig vi

On the Centre-front Line

Follow instructions for dart 1 with new horizontal line from bottom of dart to CF line. Measure initial CF line as, when gathered, the new front line should be the same.

Gathering can be adjusted when trying on garment or you may like to make up a toile first in scrap material. Match the type of fabric garment is to be made in, woven for woven, knits for knits, etc as different types of fabric can give a completely different fit.

The shoulder dart can be eliminated altogether by dividing half into different points and creating a looser fitting garment (see Chapter 12 on T-shirts).

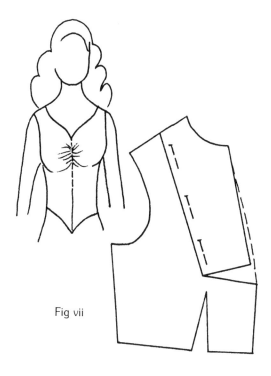

Fig vii

6 Facings

Each edge of your garment must be finished completely. This can be achieved, especially in the bodice, by facings. Figs i, ii and iii show three methods of using facings on a bodice with a yoke.

Facings should be measured 5cm (2in) from armhole and neck edges at frequent intervals (Fig i). Connect dots to make facing outline. Mark grain of fabric parallel with centre back. Trace facing to become pattern piece.

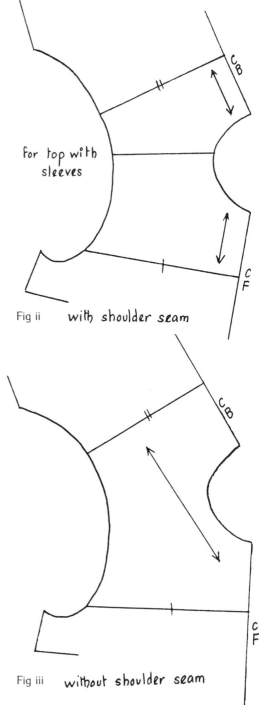

for top with sleeves

Fig ii   with shoulder seam

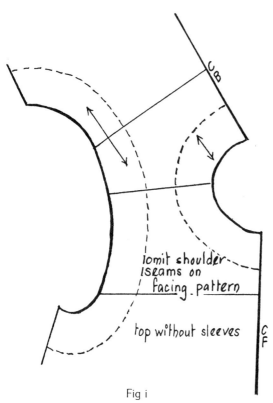

omit shoulder seams on facing pattern

top without sleeves

Fig i

NB When facings have a shoulder seam the grain lines should run parallel with centre-front and back lines (Fig ii). Follow this method for loosely woven, stretch or fine fabrics for support.

The yoke may be made in one complete piece and the grain line will depend on fabric and preference (Fig iii).

Fig iii   without shoulder seam

Facings for Buttoned Front

1 Draw around the front block.
2 The facing must be twice the width of the button stand: add 2.4cm (1in) to the centre-front line for the button stand.
3 Mark back a 5cm (2in) strip on front, curving into the shoulder line (Fig i).
4 Trace the facing piece. It can be used separately or joined to the front as one complete piece thus avoiding a seam (Fig ii).
5 For one complete front with facing use the tracing, turn over and place button stand lines to each other. Trace around complete front.

Decide on button positions. There are usually five on a blouse front.

Buttons should be placed on CF line. Buttonholes, if horizontal, should be positioned equally apart starting from the bust level for open shirts.

The buttonhole should be 0.2cm (⅛in) over CF line to accommodate button. Vertical buttonholes are placed on CF line.

See pages 46 and 120 (Rever Collars) for other facings.

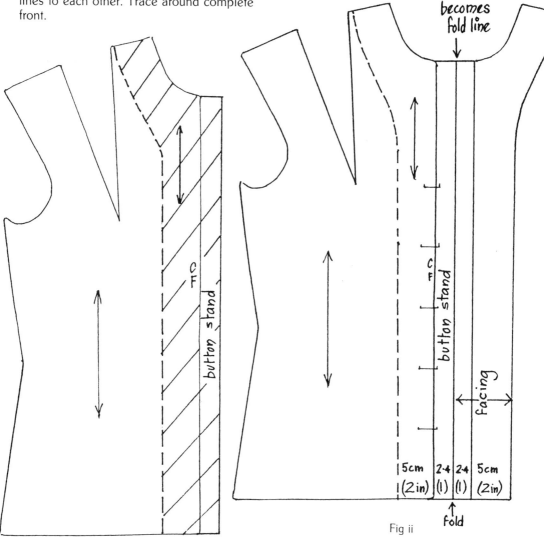

Fig i

Fig ii

7   Practice tennis dress

Procedure for Pattern Cutting

Once the basic block fits you you have enough information already to make a simple dress, top or tennis dress. Study the notes on transferring darts in Chapter 5 and facing notes in Chapter 6. The following procedure should be followed for any pattern design.

1 Draw required design.
2 Draw around front and back blocks on plain paper.
3 Fold out the shoulder dart if it is not to be used in the shoulder. Transfer dart to new position.
4 Decide on neck curve. For the tennis dress, below, mark off 1.2cm (½in) along back neckline and design the front scooped neck, making sure that you start 1.2cm (½in) into shoulder line too. Shoulder lines must be of equal length.
5 Lengthen hemline or adjust to length required.
6 Mark in facings.
7 On pattern, note:
    Centre-front and centre-back lines
    Notches (to match pieces once cut away)
    Fold lines if any
    Straight of grain lines
    Name of piece
    Number of pieces to be cut

8 Trace facings from pattern. Cut out or add seam allowances, then cut out.
9 Add seam allowances to main pattern pieces. Cut out.

NB On side seams, back and shoulder seams allow 1.6cm (⅝in). At armhole edges 0.8cm (⅜in) is sufficient as these edges will be trimmed and clipped anyway. This also applies to curved neck seams. For most hems allow 3.6cm (1½in). Beginners may find 1.6cm (⅝in) throughout easier to work with, as with commercial patterns.

Calculating Yardage

On a flat surface mark an area with two lengths of tape, half the width of fabric apart. Lay out pieces, as they will be cut, paying special attention to pieces to be placed on fold of fabric. Allow space for seam allowances if not added to pattern pieces.

Now measure along in metres (yards) the amount of fabric you will need. Any extra wide pieces may need to be cut on single fabric and should be measured separately.

Interfacing is normally sold in narrower widths so choose your interfacing ahead of time in order to make an accurate allowance.

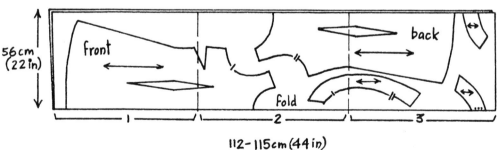

56cm (22in)

front

back

fold

1   2   3

112–115cm (44in)
wide fabric
not to scale

Tennis Dress

Style could be lengthened to regular skirt length or shortened for blouse.

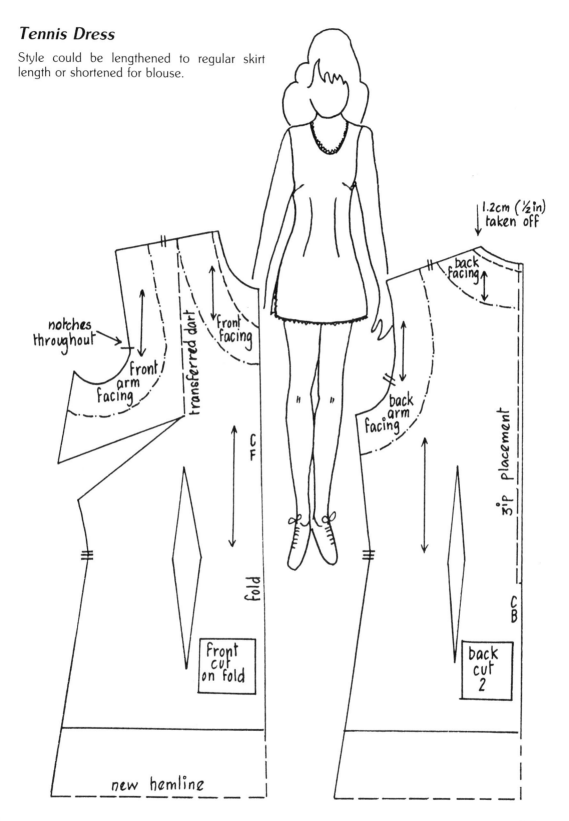

1.2cm (½ in) taken off

back facing

notches throughout

transferred dart

Front facing

Front arm facing

back arm facing

C F

Fold

zip placement

Front cut on fold

back cut 2

C B

new hemline

8 Sleeves

Basic Sleeve Blocks

The basic sleeve block is a simple straight sleeve. From this we can make a fitted sleeve, suitable for jackets. The basic sleeve is used in several variations shown later in this chapter.

You will require your sleeve measurements from Chapter 2. The measurements in the right-hand column and after each step are for the basic 91.5cm (36in) block for practice.

	yours	cm	in
Sleeve length	....	62.2	(24½)
Length to elbow	....	33	(13)
Top arm	....	33+5	(13+2)
Elbow	....	30.5	(12)
Wrist	....	17.8	(7)

1 Draw a rectangle the sleeve length × top arm measure with ease (Fig i). [62.2cm×38cm (24½in×15in)]
2 From A measure down the crown depth.

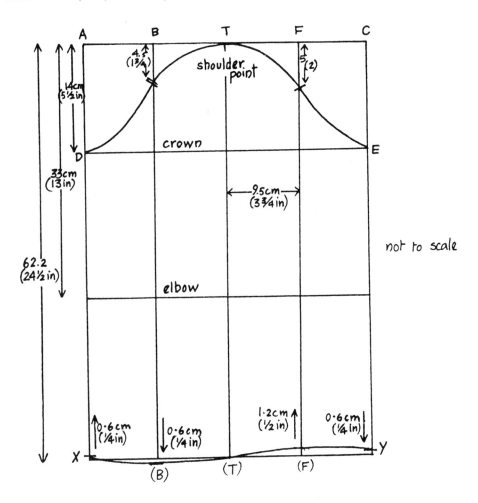

Fig i

(See chart on page 32 .) [14cm (5½in)]

3 Divide the rectangle into four lengthways. Draw in vertical lines and label across top A, B, T, F, and C. Mark a point 5cm (2in) below F and another 4.5cm (1¾in) below B. (The back sleeve crown is higher.) Draw in curved sleeve head from D, through B to T, and down through F to E.

4 Mark the sleeve to elbow line, parallel to the AC line. [33cm (13in)]

5 To shape lower edge mark a point 0.6cm (¼in) above X, 0.6cm (¼in) below B, meeting line at centre, 1.2cm (½in) above F and 0.6cm (¼in) above Y. Join up points to form curved line. Back is lower to allow for bending arm.

Fitted Sleeve

1 Draw around the sleeve (Fig i).

2 Cut up from wrist to elbow line on T line. Cut along elbow line from back to same point but not cutting through if possible. Overlap central wrist 5cm (2in) (Fig ii).

3 Re-mark central wrist. Apply required wrist measurement equally each side of centre (ie 17.8cm (7in) is 8.9cm (3½in) each side).

4 Join the new wrist point to E at front sleeve.

5 At elbow level, apply back from H, the elbow measure. Connect to D. [30.5cm (12in)]

6 Measure surplus at *, 3.6cm (1½in). Apply this measurement to other side of dart opening. Connect to wrist point at back sleeve.

7 Draw in good curved wrist line.

8 The elbow dart is usually shortened to about 7.6cm (3in). Draw a central line through dart. Mark required length of dart. Connect to original opening points at *.

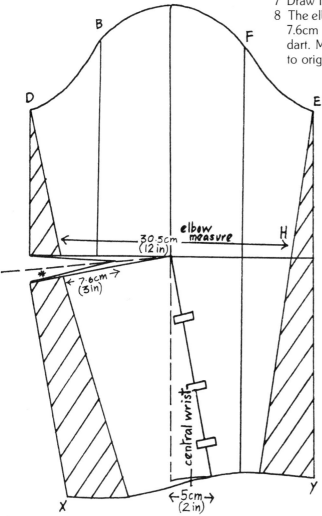

Fig ii

Sleeve Measurements

	cm	in	cm	in	cm	in	cm	in
Top arm	28	(11)	30.5	(12)	33	(13)	35.5	(14)
Sleeve size	33	(13)	35.5	(14)	38	(15)	40.6	(16)
Crown depth	12.7	(5)	13.3	(5¼)	14	(5½)	14.6	(5¾)
Elbow	29.2	(11½)	29.9	(11¾)	30.5	(12)	34.3	(13½)
Wrist	15.2	(6)	16.5	(6½)	17.8	(7)	19	(7½)
Sleeve length	56	(22)	59.7	(23½)	62.2	(24½)	64.8	(25½)
Bust	81	(32)	86.5	(34)	91.5	(36)	96.5	(38)

The sleeve sizes above are based on average measurements. Consideration should be made to the build of each individual, such as bone or muscle structure. These measurements apply to the basic straight sleeve. Different styles will greatly influence the finished look. Care should be taken to design a style that will enhance the figure type.

Cuffs

Cuffs should be made according to wrist measurement, with ease, plus 3.6cm (1½in) for the button stand. Width should be doubled. Add seam allowance.

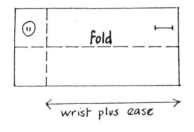

wrist plus ease

Sleeve Head

The basic sleeve head (curved line) should be 2.4–3.6cm (1–1½in) larger than the total armhole measurement of the basic toile. Measure the total armhole from the basic blocks. Measure sleeve head (Fig i, page 30). Using a flexicurve is easiest but careful use of a tape measure will suffice.

Since we know the basic block fits and adjustments were made to make an accurate armhole, the sleeve should be adjusted to fit the armhole.

(a) If sleeve head only measures 1.2cm (½in) larger than armhole:

Cut sleeve through central line (Fig ii). Open out a further 1.2cm (½in) using a paper strip under to secure. Re-draw sleeve head and wrist lines.

(b) If sleeve head measures the same or less than the armhole:

Cut through all three lines (Fig iii). Divide required measurement between three and open out. Tape down to paper strips. Re-draw sleeve head and wrist lines.

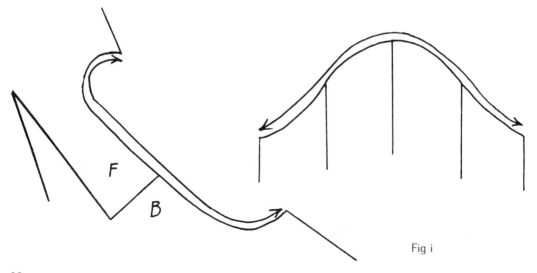

Fig i

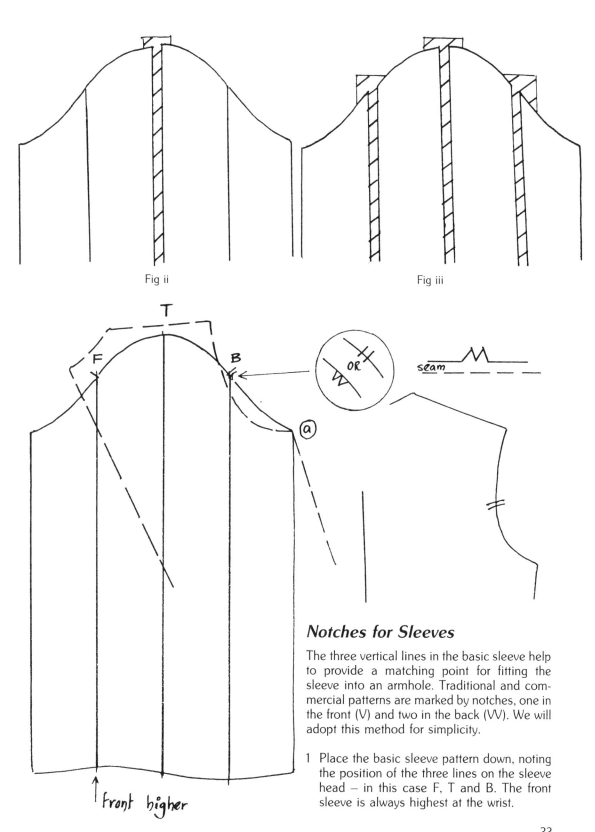

Fig ii

Fig iii

seam

Notches for Sleeves

The three vertical lines in the basic sleeve help to provide a matching point for fitting the sleeve into an armhole. Traditional and commercial patterns are marked by notches, one in the front (V) and two in the back (VV). We will adopt this method for simplicity.

1   Place the basic sleeve pattern down, noting the position of the three lines on the sleeve head – in this case F, T and B. The front sleeve is always highest at the wrist.

2 Starting with the back, place underarm point of back block to underarm point of sleeve (a). 'Walk' back block along line until it reaches point B. Mark this point on back block as B with two notches (VV). Check measurement with a flexi-curve or tape.
3 Mark front in the same manner.

The 2.4–3.6cm (1–1½in) in the sleeve head is needed between these two notched points, and is eased in when making up. 'T' (top) of the sleeve should line up with the corrected shoulder line.

When marking notches in cutting out of fabric, cut 'out' instead of 'in' to seam.

Designing Sleeves

From the basic sleeve we can create many designs. The following five styles incorporate many rules but sleeves have always offered tremendous scope of adventure in designing and you will soon want to experiment on your own.

Gathered Sleeve

This sleeve is gathered at the wrist whilst the top remains the same. The length is usually unaltered and a cuff added, providing a slight drape.

1 Draw around the basic sleeve with vertical lines.
2 Cut up lines to the top but not through.
3 Open out sleeve on lines to desired width; each opening must be equal.
4 Secure sleeve onto pattern paper and draw around.
5 Mark F and B points, position of opening and grain line.

Cuffs are cut to wrist measure, plus ease, and overlay for button. Double the width required. See notes on continuous strip openings at wrist (page 110).

T

F   B

3.6 cm
(1½in)

sleeve opening
central of
'B' line

Bishop Sleeve

The Bishop sleeve differs from the gathered sleeve by being full at both top and wrist. Like the gathered sleeve, the length is usually left unaltered with the cuff added.

1 Draw around the basic sleeve with vertical lines.
2 Draw in elbow line and mark each section 1 to 4.
3 On another piece of paper draw a horizontal line that elbow line can 'sit' on.

4 Cut out sleeve, separating each section.
5 With horizontal lines matching, lay section 1 down. Mark a 2.4cm (1in) space and lay section 2 down etc.

Each opening must be an equal division of the required size.
The sleeve head will need to be re-drawn as a dotted line. Mark F and B points, also T. These are now midway openings. Mark grain line and wrist opening (midway between B opening).

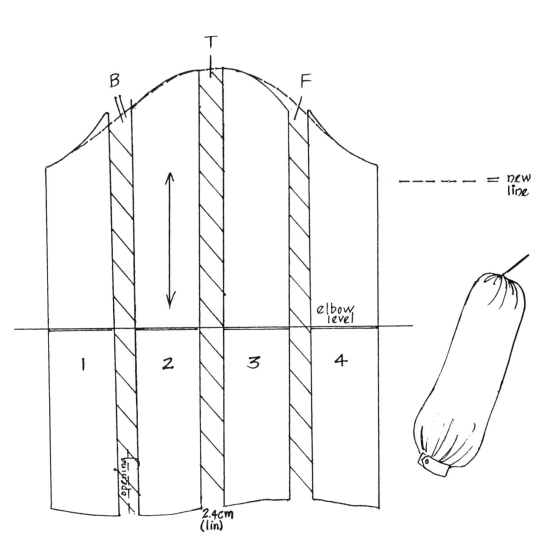

T

B

F

------- --- --- = new
line

elbow
level

1   2   3   4

Topening

2.4cm
(1in)

35

Short Flared Sleeve

Based entirely on the gathered sleeve, the short version is more likely to be wider. Often designed for lightweight fabrics, the short flare can be made in two layers, maybe one even at a different length (about 1.2–2.4cm (½–1in) difference).

Lower and top edges will need to be drawn into a smoother curve.

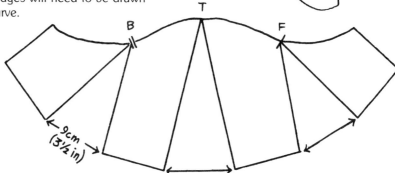

Tulip Sleeve

This sleeve is based on the short flare, with openings of 2.4cm (1in).

1 Draw around sleeve and design style lines to run through notches. Marking notches, trace one side. Cut out.

2 Cut out other side.

3 Place sides together at underarm seam lines (no seam).

4 To sew, sleeve edge should be finished first. Line up 'T' points and stitch into armhole. Sleeve can overlap to either back or front.

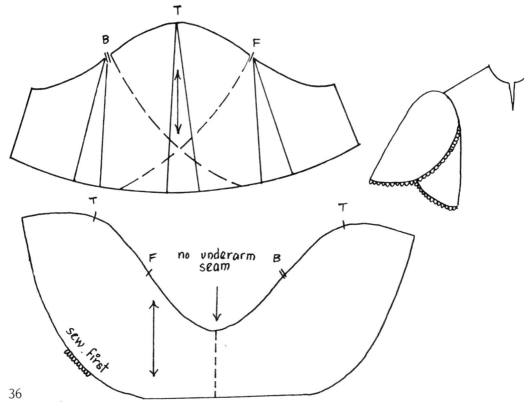

Pleated Sleeves

Pleated sleeves are usually constructed the opposite way around to the previous four designs. The sleeve head is opened out instead of the lower edge. Care should be taken to allow sufficient depth to the fold of the pleat.

1 Draw around the basic sleeve to length required.
2 Mark in three lines, B, T and F. Cut to hem.
3 Open out to size pleat. This is double to finished pleat, ie for 1.2cm (½in) pleat open out 2.4cm (1in). Secure into position.
4 Re-draw notches.

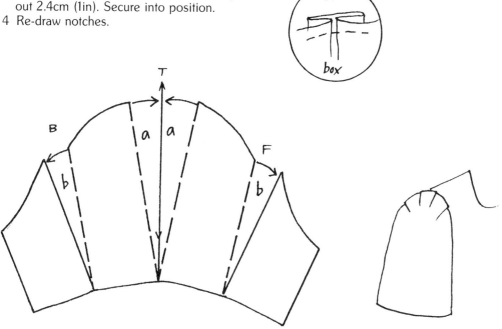

Hemline will appear straight when finished. Foldline is shown as dotted line; fold to solid line.

Pleats can be folded in or out for different effects.

This method of pleating, cutting from top to hemline, is used in other garments requiring pleating without so much fullness. It could be used for trousers, cutting from waist to ankle.

Dolman Sleeves

A very loose-style sleeve created centuries ago and still used today.

Cutting in One Piece

With straight of grain on CB, front will have a bias effect. This way of cutting calls for wider-width fabrics. Dart remains. Other sleeve-head and armhole lines are ignored.

Preparing for the Dolman

Front Transfer shoulder dart to side seam, about 3.6cm (1½in) up from waistline. Add on 1.8cm (¾in) to side seam (dart can be transferred to waistline).
Back Add on 1.8cm (¾in) to side seam.

1 Place back block on left of paper and draw around.
2 Line up front to back on shoulder line. Draw around front.
3 Position sleeve centrally, matching 'T' points.
4 Draw in new shape, curving underarm line.
5 If seam is required through shoulders, separate front from back through central line.
6 Check that underarm seams are the same in length and curve.

From this style you can then go on to construct the kimono sleeve.

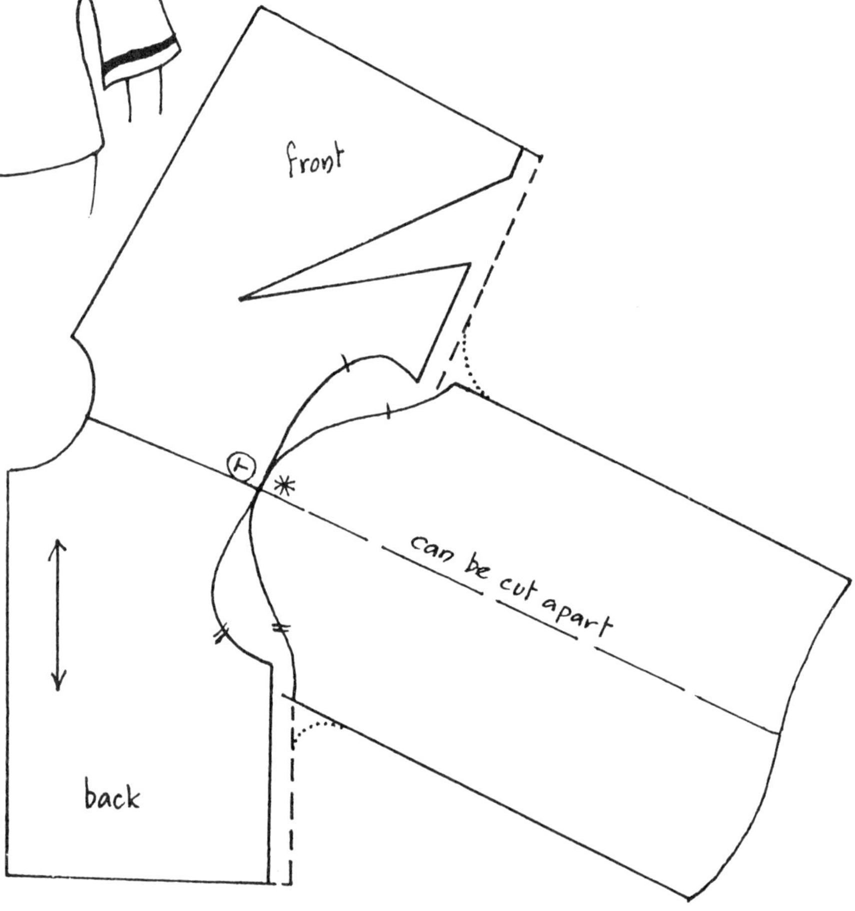

front

can be cut apart

back

Kimono Sleeves

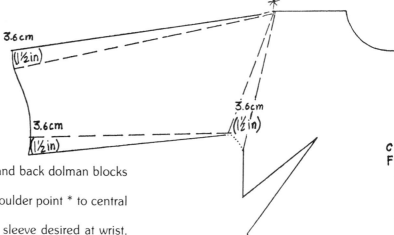

1. Draw around front and back dolman blocks separately.
2. Draw a line from shoulder point * to central underarm curve.
3. Decide on width of sleeve desired at wrist. Mark off surplus by dividing equally on both sides of sleeves.
4. Cut up underarm line to shoulder point but not through. Open out approximately the same measurement taken off at the wrist, ie if 3.6cm (1½in) is to be tapered off each sleeve side, opening should be 3.6cm (1½in).
5. Re-draw curved underarm and cut out pattern. Front and back should be alike.

Don't forget you are only dealing with half of the wrist measurement on front or back.

An opening is needed at wrist. The continuous strip method is appropriate (see Chapter 18).

Raglan Sleeves

Preparation for Construction of Raglan Sleeve

1. On the basic F, B and sleeve blocks, mark the B and F notches clearly.
2. Transfer the front shoulder dart to side. This can be moved elsewhere after construction if desired.
3. Mark centre of sleeve.

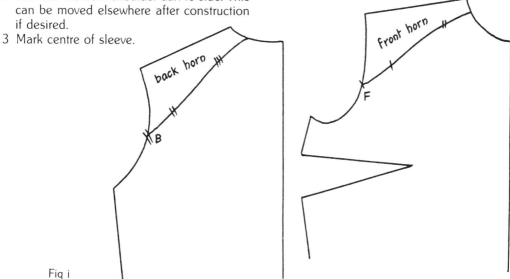

Fig i

High Raglan

1 To draw raglan lines mark a point 3.6cm (1½in) in from shoulder on neck line on both front and back blocks.

2 Connect these points to notches B and F in a slight curve.

3 Mark in notches along these lines as when the sleeve is sewn you will be putting together opposite curves and the need for notches becomes obvious. Cut away raglan 'horns'.

4 Place the basic sleeve at the bottom of your paper and mark in a 'T' at the top centre sleeve; 1.2cm (½in) above and 1.2cm (½in) to each side (Fig ii)*. Position the horns as Fig ii.

5 Let the B and F of the sleeves come as near as possible to the B and F in the armhole.

6 Mark a point 5cm (2in) down from sleeve head. With a slight curve, extend shoulder lines to touch this point.

7 If sleeve is to be cut in one piece, the shoulder seam will stop at this point and appear as a dart.

Sleeve can be cut apart with a continuous central sleeve seam.

Fig ii

high raglan

popular in sportswear
for comfort + ease

Low Raglan

In a low raglan sleeve the style lines are continued in the bodice section unlike the high raglan which stops at the notches B and F.

This style resembles the dolman style shaping but has the dividing sleeve lines. It can also be used with other styles but the basic block is an asset to your collection.

1 Draw in the style lines required on front and back blocks but ending underarm.
2 Mark notches on style lines.
3 Mark F and B.
4 Make 'T' at sleeve head, above marked central sleeve (Fig i).
5 Extend sleeve 2.4cm (1in).
6 Draw a line 2.4cm (1in) above sleeve underarm points.
7 Cut through 'horns' at regular intervals from armhole edge to style lines, up to B and F notches. Do not cut through style line (Fig ii).
8 Spread towards the new underarm point X.
9 X should be connected to existing sleeve at wrist.
10 From sleeve head mark down 5cm (2in), as on high raglan. Connect shoulder lines to this point.
11 Sleeve can be separated or cut as one with dart (as high raglan).
12 Draw around new sleeve.

Finish style to own design.

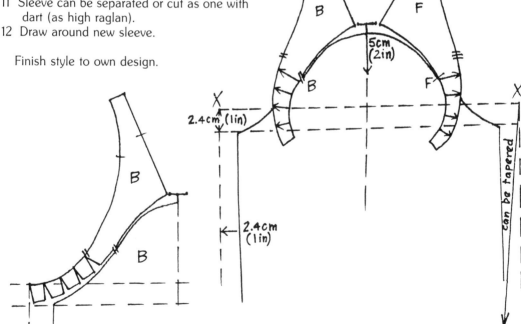

Fig i

Fig ii

9 Collars

Collars vary in measurement of the outside edge. The smaller the outside edge, the higher the collar sits. The tightness of the outside edge forces the collar to roll up the neck.

Flat Collars

There are five basic flat collars, shown below. Instructions for each are given in this chapter.

1 Peter Pan: lies completely flat

2 Eton: has slight roll

3 Roll: highest position

4 Shirt or turn-down: similar to a rever

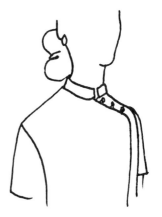

5 Mandarin: lies flat into neck

Peter Pan Collar

Use block with shoulder dart transferred to side and shoulder adjusted.

1 Outline bodice blocks, joining at shoulder lines.
2 Draw in shape of collar desired. Collar should end on centre-front line*.
3 At centre-front lower design 0.6cm (¼in) if slight roll is wanted. Lower edge of collar same amount.
4 Trace collar and cut out pattern.

Front shape can be any design and collar can be any width as it lays flat.

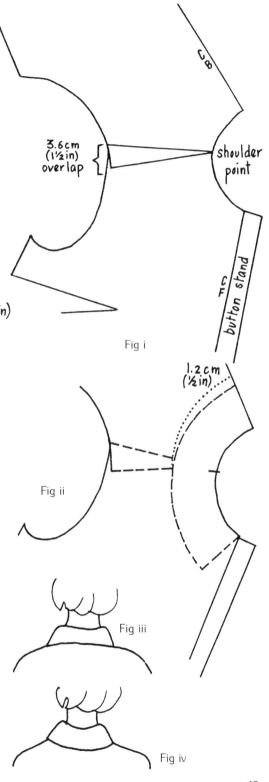

Fig i

Fig ii

Fig iii

Fig iv

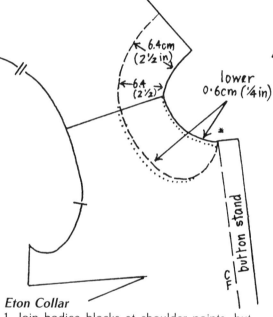

Eton Collar

1 Join bodice blocks at shoulder points, but overlapping 3.6cm (1½in) at armhole edge (Fig i).
2 Draw in collar measuring at regular intervals from neck edge. Add on 1.2cm (½in) at centre back tapering back into collar near shoulder line (Fig ii).
3 Re-draw collar. Trace and cut out pattern.

Because the outside edge of the collar has been reduced, the collar will roll slightly into the neck.

The extra length at the back prevents the collar from looking shorter. Fig iii shows the effect, minus the extra length, and Fig iv shows this rectified.

43

Roll Collar

1 Outline a flat (Peter Pan) collar and cut it out (Fig i).
2 Mark position of two darts, one (a) near the shoulder seam and the other (b) between CB and shoulder (Fig ii).
3 Fold out darts 1.8cm (¾in). Secure. For a higher fitting collar a 1.2cm (½in) dart (c) may be taken out at centre back.
4 Lower front neck 1.2cm (½in).
5 Re-draw the collar, adding 1.8cm (¾in) to centre-back length.

Front can be any design (Fig iii).

If collar is to lap over to accommodate button and buttonhole, add 3.6cm (1½in) to centre front.

Shirt or Turn-down Collar

These are tight-fitting, simple-tailored collars usually designed for shirts worn open at the neck.

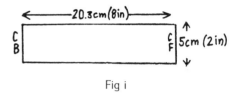

Fig i

1 Draw a rectangle half the neck measurement × 5–7.6cm (2–3in) (Fig i).
2 Mark centre back and front at each end. Mark shoulder point by measuring from neckline of basic front and back blocks. 1.2cm (½in) can be added to centre back as collar will roll up into neck, even with shirt worn open (Fig ii).

An alternative style can be achieved by adding an extra 2.4cm (1in) all the way along collar (Fig iii).

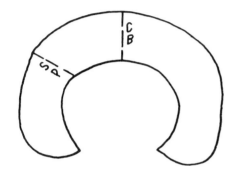

Fig i

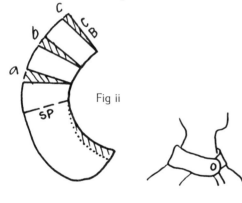

Fig ii

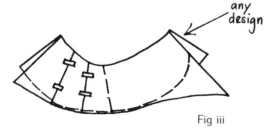

any design

Fig iii

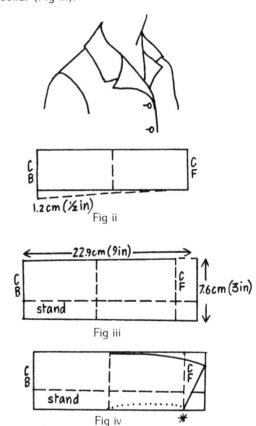

Fig ii

1.2cm (½in)

Fig iii

stand

22.9cm (9in)

7.6cm (3in)

Fig iv

stand

3 Design end of collar ending at neck point *
   (Fig iv). A slightly curved line may be
   necessary for a comfortable fit on neck
   edge.
4 Add button stands and facings to front
   pattern (Fig v).

   See Chapter 18 on construction method,
   also Chapter 14 for men's shirt collar designing.

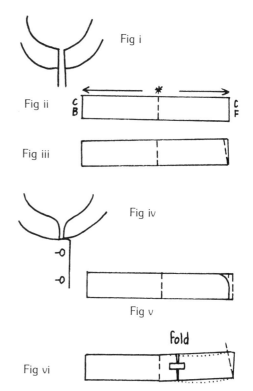

Fig i

Fig ii

Fig iii

Fig iv

Fig v

Fig vi

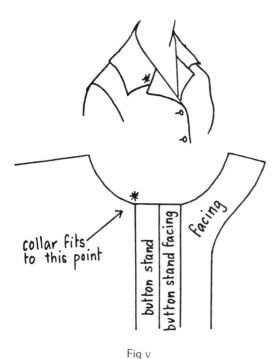

collar fits to this point

button stand

button stand facing

Facing

Fig v

Mandarin Collar

This traditional stand-up type collar is usually
2.4cm (1in) wide (Fig i).

1 Draw a rectangle the required width × half
   the neck size * (Fig i). Measure from your
   blocks. Mark centre front and back and
   shoulder point.

   The collar can be left just like this or with
   0.6cm (¼in) trimmed away at top edge (Fig
   iii). This will depend on individual neck and
   comfort. Sometimes a gap of about 1.2cm
   (½in) in front where collar usually joins will
   enhance style (Fig iv).

2 Re-shape centre front as Fig v.

   Either collar can be a closer fit in front by
folding a small dart out of front section
between shoulder point and centre front (Fig

vi). Neck edge remains the same length but
both edges can be curved slightly.

   This principle of attaching a straight piece of
fabric to a curved edge can be used to design
neckties (Fig vii). They can be any width or
length. Be sure to mark position of shoulder
points and centre back and front of tie.

   When sewing, the straight edge should be
clipped through seam allowance along piece
to be attached to neckline. Stay-stitch along
the seam allowance of the garment neckline
and clip this also to stitching (Fig viii). Baste
together and stitch.

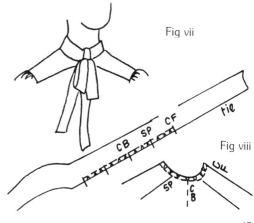

Fig vii

Fig viii

Rever Collars

Rever collars are usually designed for jackets. Before adding your collar, you may want to enlarge your basic block (see Chapter 13).

We are going to use two methods, one for a jacket without a back collar that does not fasten in front, and the other with both back collar and fastening. See also page 120.

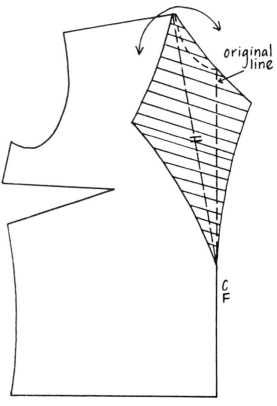

Fig ii

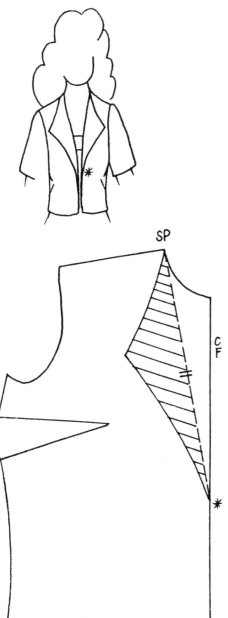

Fig i

46

Bolero Type – With No Back Collar

1 Outline front block that has dart in side.
2 Draw in the 'roll' line from shoulder point to bottom of desired collar (Fig i).* Mark notches on roll line.
3 Design collar. Draw directly on front. This style makes it very easy to see what the finished garment will look like.
4 Make a tracing of the collar only (Fig i). Cut out.
5 Matching notches, position collar along roll line as Fig ii. By drawing around the whole new front, this pattern piece becomes the front and undercollar.

It is now necessary to make a facing and top collar for this and these can be designed as one piece.
6 To make the front facing, top collar and back facing in one, first draw around the new front pattern (Fig ii).
7 Place back into position matching shoulder lines (Fig iii).

8 Mark facing 5cm (2in) away from neck and centre-front edge.
9 Draw in curve from shoulder to front*.
10 Note straight of grain, parallel with centre front. Trace and cut out pattern piece.

Facing becomes top collar and folds under at back and lower front as facings (Fig iv).

Be sure to use a good interfacing on collars. It should be attached to the facings and not garment piece. Choose stretch interfacings for stretch fabrics and woven for woven fabrics. Iron-on interfacings, available in both types, save time.

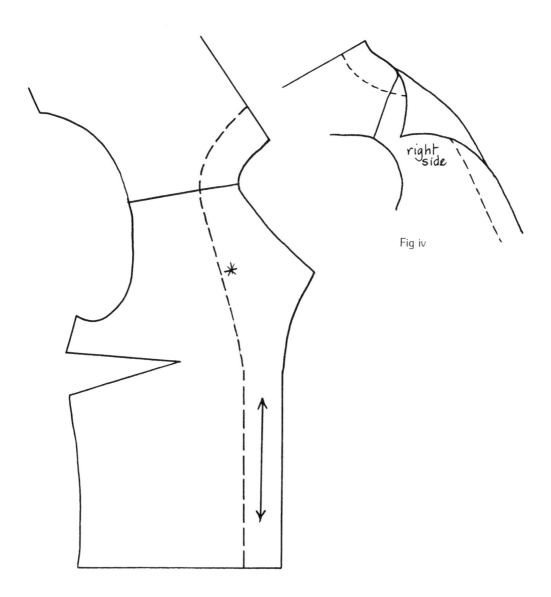

Fig iv

Fig iii

Rever Complete with Back Collar

1 Draw around the front block with side dart.
2 Add 2.4cm (1in) to centre front for button stand.
3 Draw in roll line from shoulder point to bottom of desired collar*, on right side of button stand. Extend line approximately 7.6cm (3in) beyond shoulder point (Fig i).
4 Position back block as Fig i, with shoulders touching. The centre back must touch the extended roll line ø.

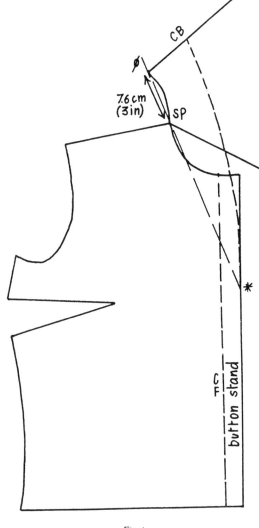

Fig i

5 Design collar from centre back to *. Collar should be deeper in the back to allow for roll.
6 Trace around new front to become the front and undercollar (see Fig ii).
7 Trace the new front and undercollar as one piece.
8 Measure in approximately 7.6cm (3in) from centre-front line to a point 5cm (2in) into the shoulder line. Connect, to form facing line.

When lining a jacket, the amount left in this front after the facing is cut away becomes the lining pattern.

The facing becomes the top collar and has a join in the back.

Back lining is same as garment back with 2.4cm (1in) pleat added to centre-back line for ease.

Don't forget to add seam allowances to facing/lining line.

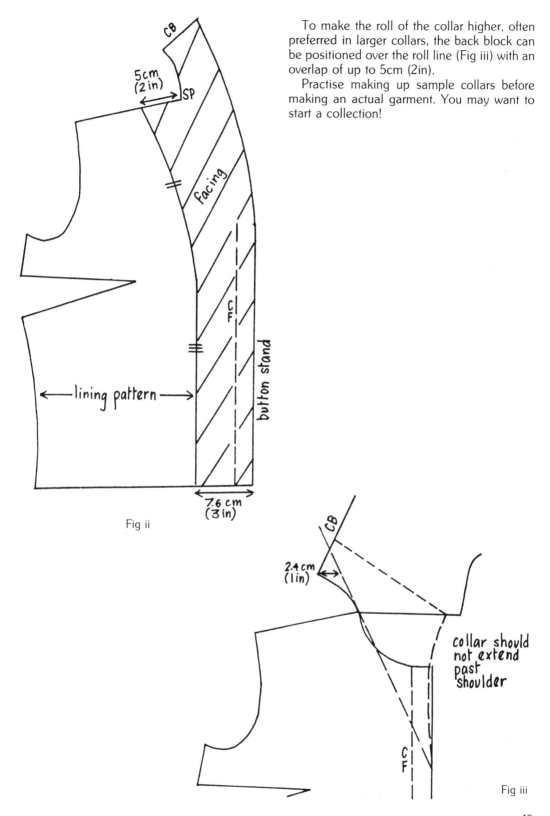

To make the roll of the collar higher, often preferred in larger collars, the back block can be positioned over the roll line (Fig iii) with an overlap of up to 5cm (2in).

Practise making up sample collars before making an actual garment. You may want to start a collection!

CB

5cm
(2in)

SP

facing

C
F

lining pattern

button stand

7.6 cm
(3 in)

Fig ii

CB

2.4 cm
(1 in)

collar should
not extend
past
shoulder

C
F

Fig iii

Cowl Neckline

Often achieved by draping fabric onto a model, rather than flat pattern method, this neckline is not really a collar and is very simple to construct.

1 Draw a line to centre front from bottom of shoulder dart, on front block (Fig i).
2 Close shoulder dart and open out on new line by cutting across to bottom of dart (Fig ii).
3 Re-draw centre-front line. Draw a horizontal line from * to shoulder point (Fig ii). This completes the front pattern but for easy sewing it is best to add a facing.
4 Draw in facing line from a point 7.6cm (3in) on shoulder line to new centre-front line (Fig ii). Mark notches on top line*.
5 Trace facing on paper. Cut out. Lining up notches, position facing piece on top line as Fig ii.
6 Draw around entire front.

Facing will be folded to inside and stitched into shoulder seam. It will not be necessary to sew down the edge as this style is supposed to drape freely.

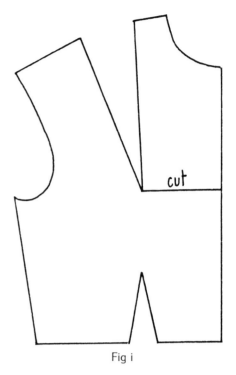

Fig i

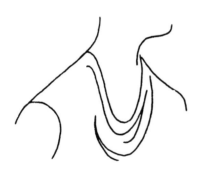

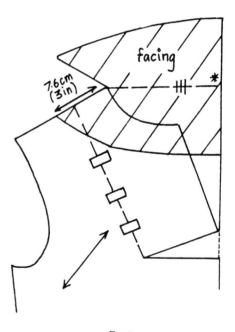

Fig ii

Built-up Neckline

The built-up neckline gives the appearance of a high collar but has no joining seam. It is a very flattering style especially when wanting to 'add length' to a short neck.

Back
1 Draw around the back block to the waist.
2 Make a new centre-back line, 0.6cm (¼in) out at neck and 0.6cm (¼in) in at waist line.
3 At neck edge, on new centre-back line, mark a point 2.4cm (1in) up.
4 Mark a point 2.4cm (1in) from shoulder to A.
5 Draw curved line from centre back to A. From A, slope a line into shoulder at B, approximately 3.2cm (1¼in) from shoulder point.

Front
1 Draw around the front block to waist with side dart.
2 Make a new centre-front line the same as centre back.
3 Transfer the side dart, in part, to the neck edge. Draw a line from end of side dart to neckline. Cut through centre of side dart to end and from neckline to same point without cutting through. Open out neckline to form a 1.8cm (¾in) dart, thus closing the side dart a little.
4 Raise shoulder point 2.4cm (1in) as back, and sloping into the shoulder in the same way, C to D. From C, slope the neckline to centre front. This will depend on individual neck and should be designed for comfort.

The waist is now smaller due to the slant required in the centre-back and front lines. Adjust at waist darts by reducing them 0.6cm (¼in). If darts are not being used, adjust difference at side seams.

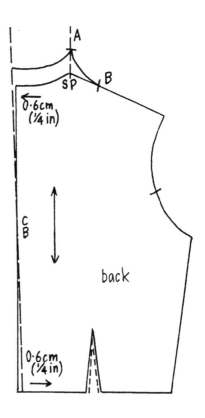

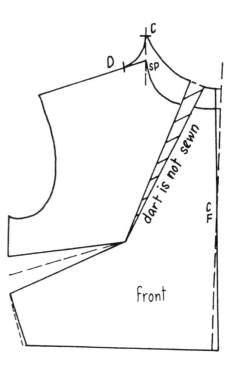

51

10 Skirts

Basic Skirt Block

The basic skirt block can be used separately or with the bodice block. In Fig i an 'A' line skirt has been incorporated into the basic straight design which can be traced off. The only measurements you will need will be waist, hips and length.

Fig i shows a basic 91.5cm (36in) block and the figures for this will be shown in square brackets after each step.

Basic Straight Design
1 AB = skirt length. Draw A and B lines across paper horizontally. [61cm (24in)]
2 Mark a point C 20.3cm (8in) below A for hip line.
3 CD = half the hip measurement plus 2.4cm (1in) ease. Complete rectangle. [52cm (20½)]
4 Mark a point E midway between CD line. Draw in vertical central line from X through E to Z. [26cm (10¼in)]
5 From top left of paper, on back, measure along a quarter of the waist plus 3.6cm (1½in) for dart to a point F. Raise F 1.2cm (½in). [17.8+3.6 = 21.4cm (7+1½ = 8½in)]
6 Connect F to E in curved line. This is the side seam.
7 Mark a point midway between AF for dart. Mark 1.8cm (¾in) each side. Draw centre dart line down 15.2cm (6in). Connect each side of dart to side points at waist points A and F in curved lines.

8 Lower A 0.6cm (¼in). Draw in waist line from dart sides to A and F.
9 Measure along from centre front, at waist level, a quarter of the waist plus 2.4cm (1in) ease. [20.3cm (8in)]
10 Raise this point, G, 1.2cm (½in). Join G to E in matching curve to back.
11 Lower waist on centre front 1.2cm (½in).
12 Mark midway point from centre front to G. Mark points 1.2cm (½in) each side to indicate waist pleat. This can be made into a dart if preferred but should be shorter than the back dart. Either, pleat or dart, can be made smaller to allow ease.
13 Connect each side of dart or pleat to side point G and centre front at waist in curved lines. This completes the straight skirt.

'A'-line Skirt
1 Mark a point 3.6cm (1½in) each side of point Z. Call these H and J.
2 Connect H and J to E.

The 'A'-line patterns should be traced from the block (shaded). The back side seam runs from F, through E to J. The front side seam runs from G, through E to H. The side seams of the skirt may require shaping at H and J, but this can be done at the fitting stage and indicated on pattern later.

Waistbands should be straight. Draw a rectangle the waist length, plus any ease, plus 3.6cm (1½in) for button stand, x double the finished width (see Fig ii).

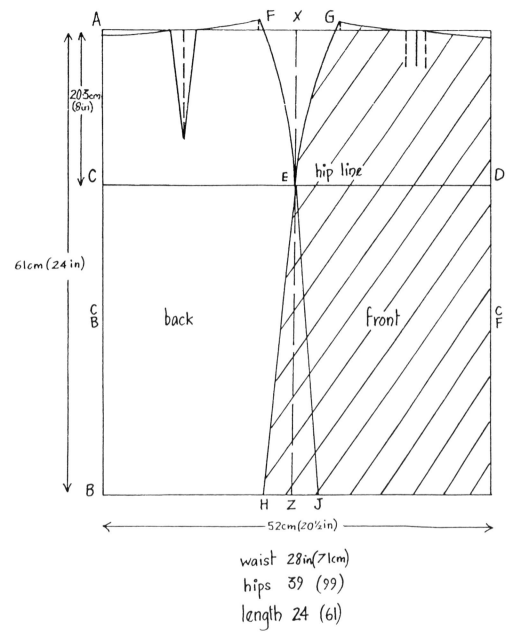

A   F   X   G

20·3cm (8in)

61cm (24in)

C   E   hip line   D

C
B   back   front   C
F

B   H   Z   J

52cm(20½in)

waist 28in(71cm)
hips 39 (99)
length 24 (61)

Fig i   Basic skirt

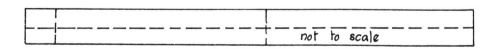

not to scale

Fig ii

Flared Skirt

The basic 'A'-line skirt can be used to make a more flared version by simply adding more width to the hemline. We do this by dividing the amount required equally between four pieces (two each half).

1 Measure the lower edge of both front and back skirts. In Fig iii the total back would measure 58.4cm (23in) and, presuming the same measurement for the front, this would mean an all-round measurement of 116.8cm (46in). By making eight divisions in the skirt (four in both front and back of 6.3cm (2½in) each) we could add 50.4cm (20in). The total hemline would then measure 167.2cm (66in).
2 Divide front and back basic skirt blocks into three vertically (Fig iii).

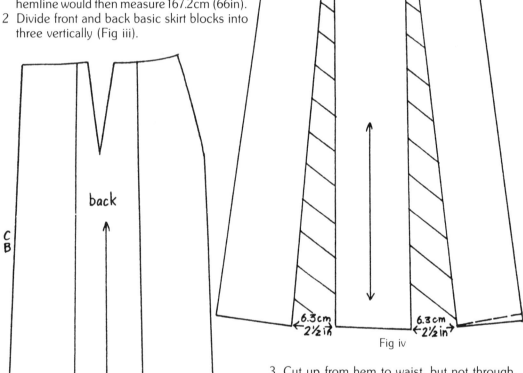

back

C
B

'A' line

Fig iii

6.3cm
2½in

6.3cm
2½in

Fig iv

3 Cut up from hem to waist, but not through. Open out each section 6.3cm (2½in).
4 Trace pattern. The hemline will require shaping at side seams. This can be done at the fitting stage and any alteration applied to the pattern later.
Note grain lines.

54

Panelled Skirts

A panelled skirt can be constructed from any basic skirt block, but usually the flared type (Fig iii) is used. It is helpful to use the division lines that were made when opening out the original block to make the flare*.

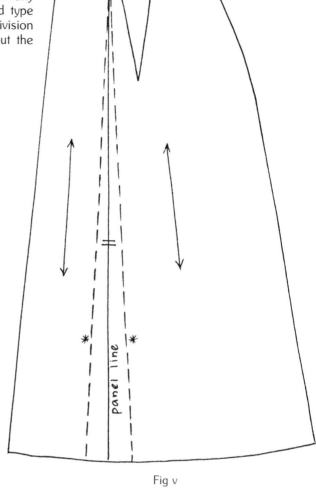

Fig v

Fig vi

Since a six-panel skirt requires three panels each in the front and back, we will use the centre-front and centre-back lines as fold lines when constructing. Any zip should be put into the side seam.

Draw in the style line for the central panel at one third of the block. This can be done by tracing the division lines on the flared block * and drawing the panel line centrally to these (Fig v). Alternately, divide the panels under the dart, thus eliminating the dart altogether (Fig vi).

The dart could also be moved towards the centre, corresponding with the style line in Fig v. Always mark panels with notches before separating.

Panelled skirts with Pleats

To add pleats to a panel, first decide on the length and depth of pleat desired. The pleated extension is always twice the width of the finished appearance of the pleat.

Draw the rectangular extension at right angles to seam line of panel.

Mark notches on panel seams and pleats. This type of pleating requires top-stitching into position either slanted or straight (see insert*). The pleat can be extended all the way up to the waist but is often bulky.

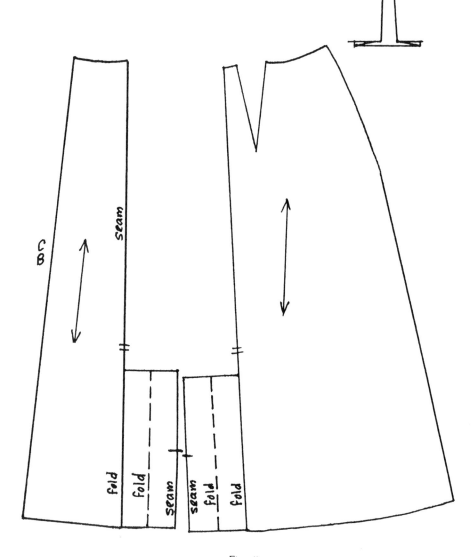

Fig vii

Front-inserted Pocket

A front-inserted pocket can also be added to any of the basic skirt blocks.

1 On the front pattern draw in any desired shape of pocket, making allowance for one's hand to fit in.
2 Draw around a depth line around the pocket, about 20.3cm (8in) in from waist. This will not be seen on the skirt but becomes the inner pocket. Mark notches.

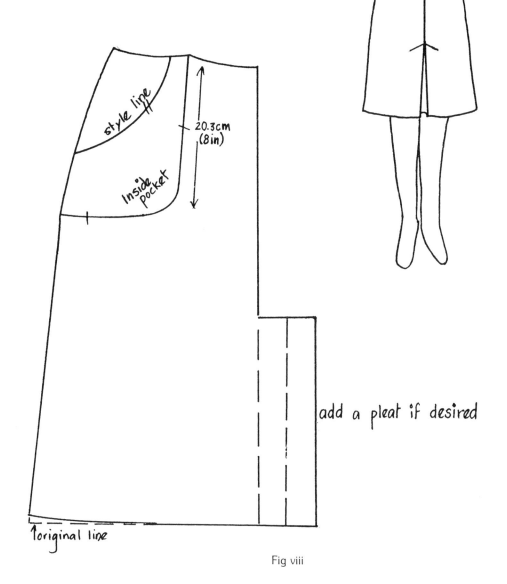

20.3cm (8in)

style line

Inside pocket

original line

add a pleat if desired

Fig viii

3 Trace the pocket shape (a). This becomes the inner pocket and is cut in the same fabric as skirt.
4 Trace shape (b) to make lining. This is attached first to the skirt at the style line.
5 Cut skirt pattern away at style line, making (c).

See Chapter 17 for construction method and other pocket ideas.

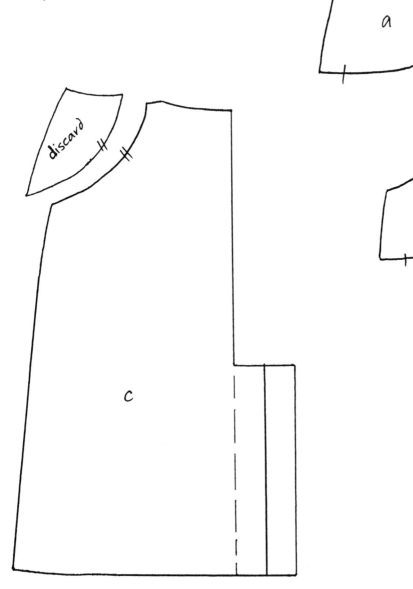

Fig ix

Half-circle Skirt

The half-circle skirt does not require a basic skirt block. Make sure you have enough paper to construct the pattern. You will need a square approximately your skirt length plus one third waist measurement. Design shown is for a 63.5cm (25in) waist with a skirt length of 61cm (24in).

1 Take away 2.4cm (1in) from actual waist measurement. Bias skirts do not require ease.
2 At top left of paper measure down the radius of the new waist measure ie waist divided by three. From same point measure across the same distance. [20.3cm (8in)]
3 Draw in the quarter circle to become half of the waist line.
4 From this curved waist line, measure down, at regular intervals, the skirt length and mark each point. Connect points to form the curved hemline. Pattern would be cut twice in fabric.

If you have difficulty in purchasing fabric in width required for this pattern, the pattern may be divided in half, thus making another version of a panelled skirt with four panels.
5 Mark straight of grain lines and notches on seam lines.

See Chapter 18 for sewing tips on curved hems.

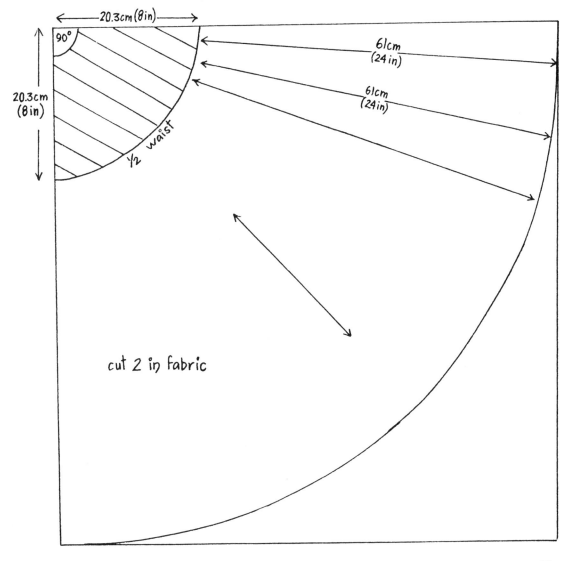

11 Trousers

Many trousers do not fit because of an inaccurate crotch length. To take this measurement, sit on a level chair and, with a tape measure, measure from waist, around hip curve, to chair. Add 2.4cm (1in) for ease. Make a note of measurement. You will also need waist, hips, outside leg length and length from waist to knee. Measurements in square brackets after each step are for the basic 91.5cm (36in) block.

	cm	in
Waist . . . add 2.4cm (1in) ease	73.6	(29)
Hips . . . no ease	99	(39)
Crotch length...............................	32.9	(13)
Outside leg	101.5	(40)
Waist to knee...............................	58.4	(23)

Trouser Block

1. Approximately 25.4cm (10in) down from top of paper and 20.3cm (8in) in from left, draw a horizontal line, AB, half the hip measurement. [49.5cm (19½in)]
2. Square up to waist level 20.3cm (8in). Draw across C to D. (Use individual measurement.)
3. From waist, measure down the crotch level and the outside leg measurement. Complete the rectangle, noting waist, hip, crotch and hem lines. [33cm (13in) 101.5cm (40in)]
4. Mark a central vertical line.
5. At waist level, mark off 3.6cm (1½in) each side of central line. Raise each point 1.2cm (½in). Draw in side-seam curves from raised point down approximately 15.2cm (6in).
6. On right, the front, mark a central point for pleat. Mark 1.2cm (1in) each side. Lower centre front 1.2cm (½in) at waist (Fig ii).

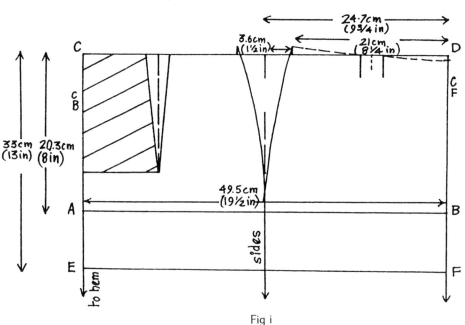

Fig i

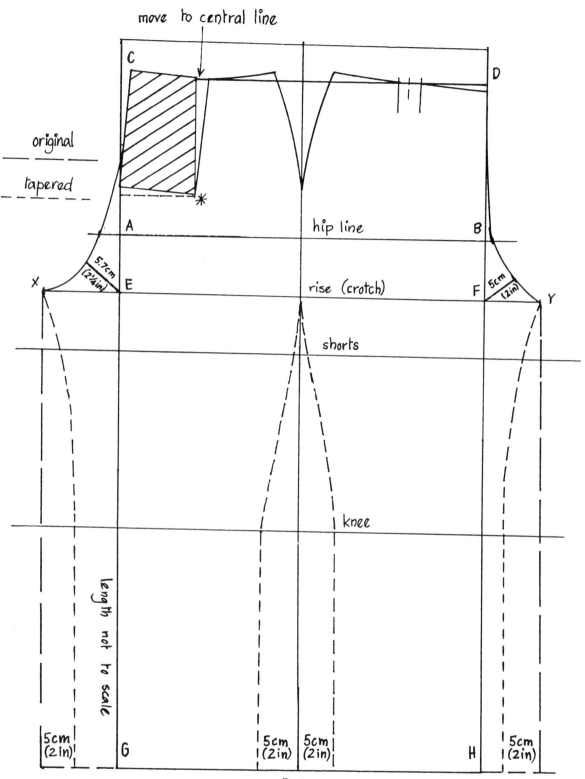

move to central line

original

tapered

C

D

hip line

A

B

5.7cm
(2¼in)

rise (crotch)

E

F

5cm
(2in)

X

Y

shorts

knee

length not to scale

5cm
(2in)

5cm
(2in)

5cm
(2in)

5cm
(2in)

G

H

Fig ii

Draw in curved waistline as for skirts. The pleat can be made into a dart and should be shorter that the back dart.

7 Mark the central point of the back waist. The dart size depends on the difference between amount in waist now and amount needed. Measure the front, deducting amount in pleat [18.4cm (7¼in)]. Measure the back [21cm (8¼in)]. Add together [39.4cm (15½in)]. Deduct half the required waist measure away from this [36.8cm (14½in)]. The difference is approximately 2.4cm (1in). This is the necessary dart size.

8 Mark a point 15.2cm (6in) below waist on central line *. Mark 1.2cm (½in) points each side. Connect points to form the back waist dart.

9 Cut pattern on a horizontal line from centre back to bottom of dart, and from waist down left dart line to same point without cutting through*. To reduce the dart and create a sloping back seam, move left dart line over to central dart line (Fig ii). Tape down.

10 Draw in the back curved waistline. Following Fig ii, extend E 10.2cm (4in), F 7.6cm (3in), A 2.4cm (1in) and B 1.2cm (½in). The crotch curves are drawn through these points. They are average measurements and should be adjusted to the individual (see Chapter 15 on adjusting children's trousers. Corrections can be made to create the same body shape as the individual.

11 At E draw a line bisecting the angle 5.7cm (2¼in).

12 At F draw in a 5cm (2in) bisecting line. Draw in curved crotch lines.

13 For straight-leg trousers draw lines down from X and Y to hem line. These can turn out fairly wide, especially on larger hip sizes, but can be tapered to individual style. Most tapering is shaped from the thigh, but should be taken out equally between inside and outside seams on any style (Fig ii).

14 Draw in knee level and short level.

Shorts

Shorts can be any length desired. They are often curved at the side for comfort. It is often a good idea to make up the trouser block as shorts as it could be less wasteful in the event of alterations. Always use woven fabric as knits give a false sense of fit.

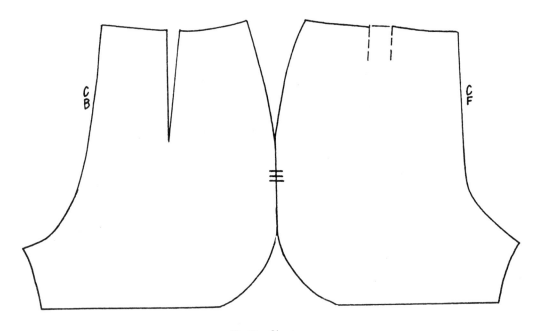

Fig iii Shorts

Culottes

Culottes require the basic skirt and basic trouser patterns combined. The solid line indicates the trouser pattern and the dotted line, the skirt pattern.

1 Draw around the basic trouser pattern to the knee (front and back are designed in the same way). Position basic skirt as diagram below. Line up waist levels on CB and CF lines.
2 Trace the trouser pattern to the point where it touches the CB or CF skirt lines. Use skirt darting and waist line.
3 Add a pleat to the CB and CF skirt lines. (Pleat notes are covered in Chapter 10.)
4 Re-position traced slack piece to the other side of pleat. Draw around complete culotte patterns.
5 Culottes are usually short for sportswear but can also be skirt length or Bermuda short length.

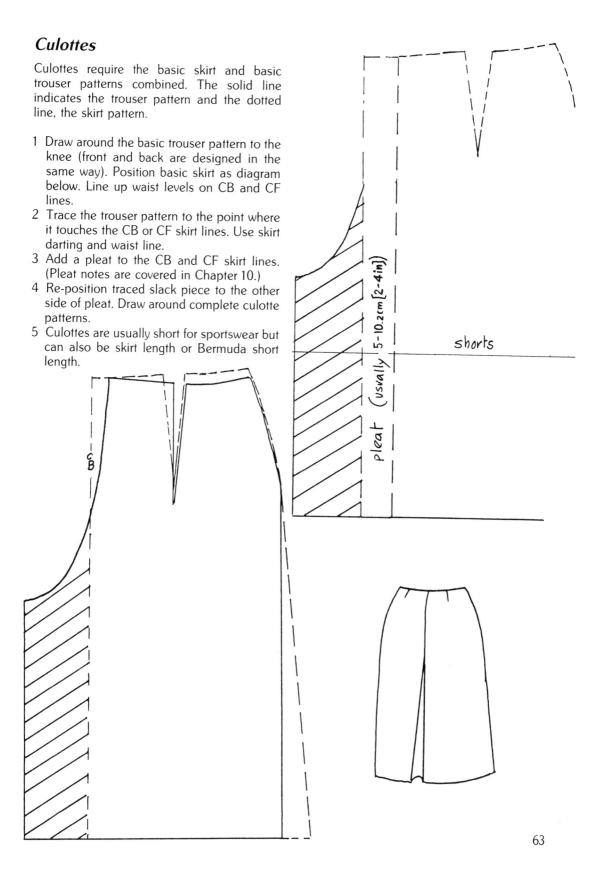

shorts

pleat (usually 5-10.2cm [2-4in])

CB

12 Variations

Princess Line

A very flattering style for larger figure types, the princess line adds length. The vertical lines create an illusion of height. Darts are used within style lines on the basic block resulting in an excellent fit.

The princess line dress is usually made up of seven panels, the centre front not having a seam.

Front

1 Draw around the front block to the hip line.
2 Mark bust and waist level, plus a mid-bust line between original bust line and top of waist dart.
3 Extend hip line to length required on centre-front line. Apply the same measurement to the sloping side seam. Re-draw hemline sloping at side.
4 Draw in a central dart line vertically through waist dart to bust point, at dart end (Fig i). Mark a point 3.6cm (1½in) either side of line at hem. This measurement can be smaller or up to 6.3cm (2½in) larger depending on flare desired. The side seam slope should be adjusted too.
5 From left side of dart, draw a line to point B and connect right side to A.
6 On centre bust line (dotted), lengthen shoulder and waist darts to touch *. The side section is sometimes more curved. Remember that the basic block from which this was constructed allows 5cm (2in) ease around the bust. Fig 1 shows the new style line taking away some of this ease. Design shape to individual taste.
7 Mark notches on new lines to help when sewing.
8 Trace each section separately, drawing a curve at bust and waist if desired (see Fig ii).
9 Front panel is cut in one piece. Mark centre front to be cut on the fold of fabric.
10 Hem is usually curved at side seam, approximately 0.6cm (¼in).

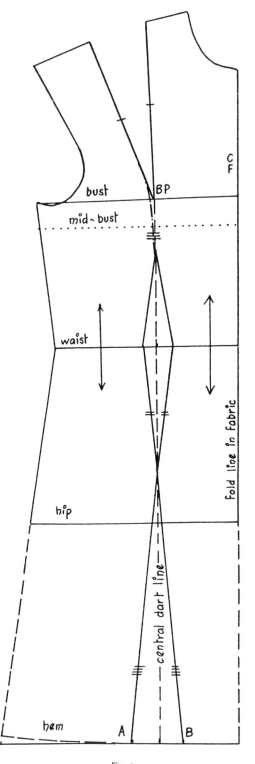

Fig i

side front

front

cut on fold

Fig ii

65

Back

1 Draw around back block extending to hem, matching front.
2 Draw in vertical line to hem at D through centre of dart.
3 From front measure from shoulder point (SP) to style line separating the panels. On Fig iii this is 7.5cm (3in). Mark this point C.
4 Mark points E and F 3.6cm (1½in) each side of vertical line at hemline.
5 Connect style lines, making a curved line from top of dart to shoulder at C. Left side of lower dart connects to E; right side to F.
6 Mark notches and straight of grain.
7 Trace panels separately.

CB is usually a seam that will incorporate the zip opening.
NB For a looser fitting princess line the waist darts can be reduced before construction.

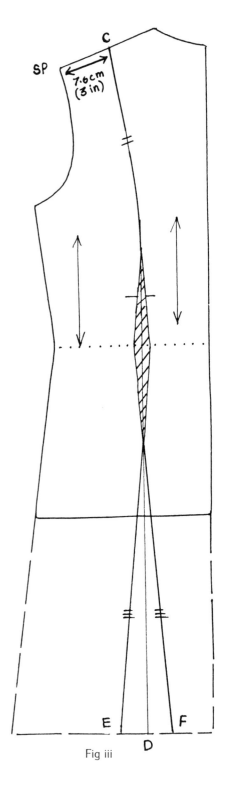

Fig iii

Sundress from Basic Princess Block

Front

1 Draw around the princess front block to waist.
2 Design top band of sundress, usually 5cm (2in) wide (see Fig i). For comfort, band should start 2.4cm (1in) below armhole at side.
3 On each side of shoulder dart lines draw in 2.4cm (1in) parallel lines to form straps.
4 Mark notches on top band and straps (Fig i).

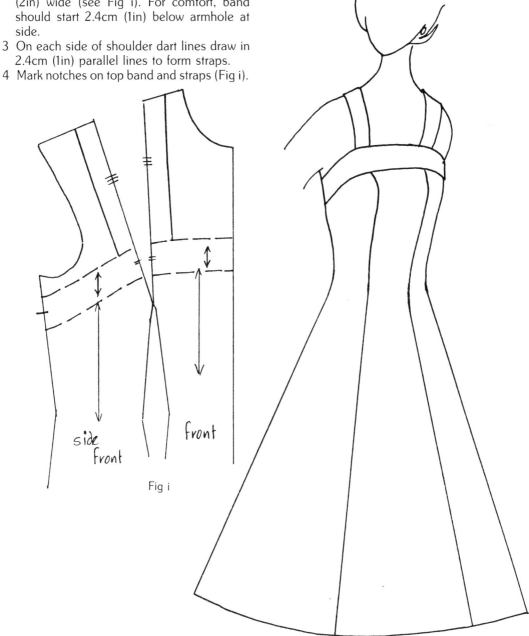

side front

front

Fig i

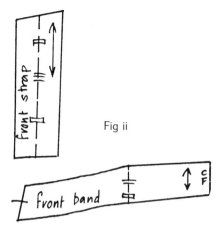

Fig ii

5 Trace band and straps. Tape together each side of straps matching notches. Tape together band pieces. Mark CF and grain lines (Fig ii).
6 Trace lower skirt from basic princess block using new style lines.

Back

The back is constructed as the front with straps drawn either side of dart to shoulder line (Fig iii). Check that straps and underarm points line up with front.

There will be a seam along shoulder line in straps which gives an excellent fit. Many dresses of this type, especially shop-bought ones, use straight straps or ribbons. Unless the shoulders are absolutely square the straps will obviously slide off the shoulder slope.

When cutting out for sewing allow enough fabric to cut straps and top band double. The straps can then be enclosed into the band lining and will look much neater.

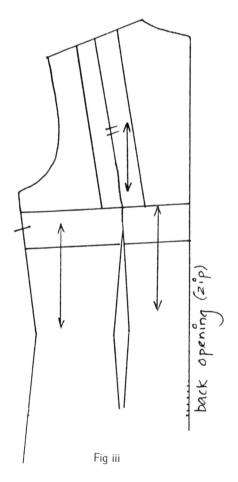

Fig iii

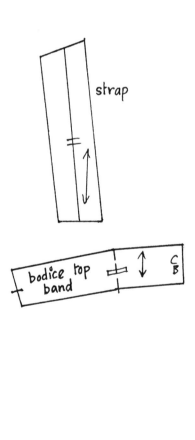

Dropped Shoulder Line

This style incorporates part of the sleeve head into the bodice blocks. Fig i shows the basic block. Any further designing, ie gathered sleeves, is added afterwards. Not suitable for broad shoulders.

This block can be used for 'off the shoulder' designs; the style line then becomes the garment top line.

1 At bottom of paper, draw around the basic sleeve to length desired.
2 Mark F and B points.
3 Draw vertical central line.
4 At top of sleeve mark a point 1.2cm (½in) above and to each side of this point, forming a 'T' *.

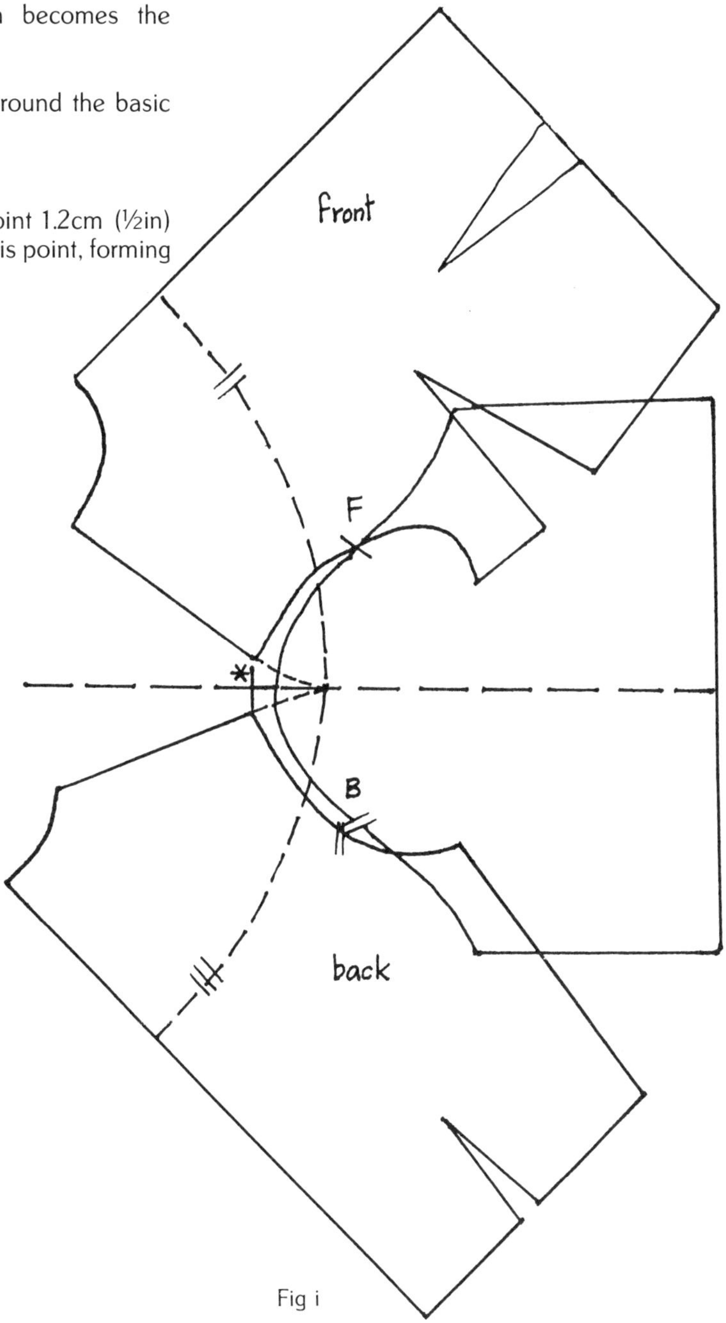

Front

F

*

B

back

Fig i

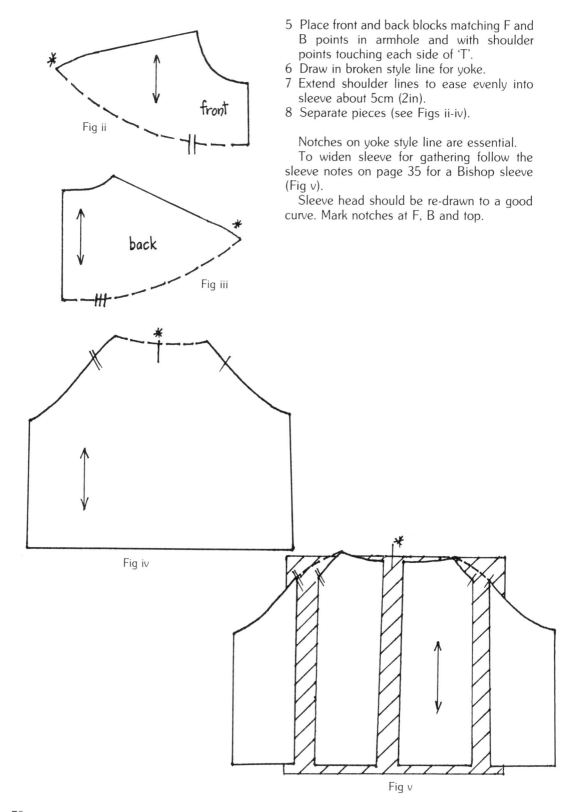

5 Place front and back blocks matching F and B points in armhole and with shoulder points touching each side of 'T'.
6 Draw in broken style line for yoke.
7 Extend shoulder lines to ease evenly into sleeve about 5cm (2in).
8 Separate pieces (see Figs ii-iv).

Notches on yoke style line are essential.
To widen sleeve for gathering follow the sleeve notes on page 35 for a Bishop sleeve (Fig v).
Sleeve head should be re-drawn to a good curve. Mark notches at F, B and top.

Fig ii

front

back

Fig iii

Fig iv

Fig v

Yokes

Yokes can add variety to any style and be an asset in creating illusions away from figure problems. For example, a narrow-shouldered, heavy-busted figure would benefit from a straight yoked bodice with soft gathering over the bustline. The horizontal line of the yoke gives width to the shoulders and takes attention away from the bustline. Extra fullness could be added into the garment for comfort in the bust area.

Often patterned fabrics can be used for effect by cutting the yokes on the bias. This looks particularly nice in plaids and checks (ie lumberjack-style shirts).

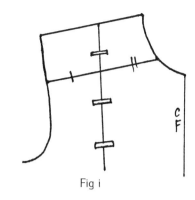

Fig i

1 Decide on the depth of the yoke.
2 Close the shoulder dart on front (Fig i).
3 Draw in yoke style line. Straight yokes can run parallel to shoulder line or with curve across chest line.
4 Mark notches.
5 Cut yoke away.
6 Open out lower front dart. This can still be used as a dart, transferred to the side, or gathered by ignoring dart lines completely (Fig ii). If to be gathered, extend gathering each side of dart lines.
7 For a fuller top, open out bodice about 2.4cm (1in) vertically.
8 Design back omitting dart procedure. If gathering is desired in back, open out lower section 2.4–5cm (1–2in) after cutting away yoke (Fig iii).

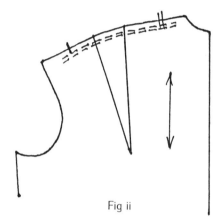

Fig ii

Yokes are usually cut double. Seams can then be enclosed between top and bottom yoke.

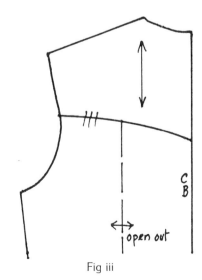

Fig iii

71

T-shirts

For a basic T-shirt there is no need for darts. The following basic block is referred to as a semi-fit as we are not eliminating all the dart shaping. Use the basic block or the reduced block, as in lingerie (see Chapter 16), for a closer fit.

1 Draw around the front block with shoulder dart.
2 Divide shoulder dart in half (Fig i).
3 Draw line from bottom of dart into armhole (Fig ii).

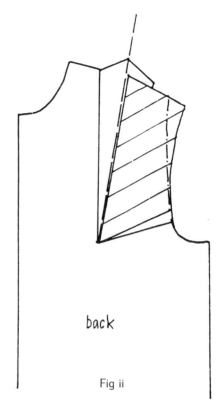

back

Fig ii

4 Close out dart, dividing half into armhole and half to shoulder (Fig ii). Ignore waist darts.
5 Connect underarm point to hip with a straight line.
6 To draw in new armhole, measure correct shoulder length from back block, as using only half of the dart has lengthened shoulder. Mark this point. Draw in new armhole with a curved line (Fig ii).
7 Trace block with NO darts.
8 Trace the back block, eliminating dart and straightening side seam.

The neck may be lowered and widened according to style required. (See page 123 for construction of 'Tab' front, popular in men's T-shirts.)

Ribbing for T-shirts

Use single- or double-loop knit fabrics and cut with grain up and down body.

Pre-wash every type of knit: leave tube-knitted types uncut until after washing. Allow 0.6cm (¼in) seams throughout.

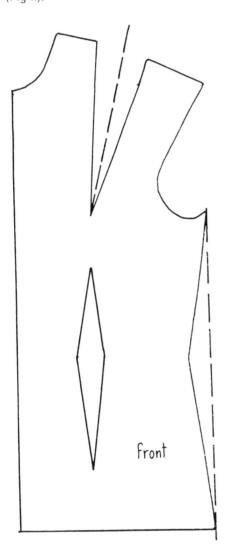

front

Fig i

To measure sleeve and neck ribbing bands

1 Measure finished edge of garment sleeve and neck.
2 Fold ribbing in half lengthways to desired width (usually 5cm (2in) which makes a 1.8cm (¾in) band (Fig i).
3 Hold ribbing at end of measure, gently stretch to required length. Add 1.2cm (½in) for seam and cut measured piece.
4 Try neck ribbing over head to ensure fit allows for pulling on.

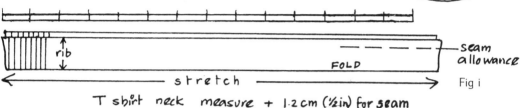

Fig i

T shirt neck measure + 1.2cm (½in) for seam

To Make up T-shirt

1 Make one shoulder seam (Fig ii).
2 Treating total neck as one unit, divide into 4. Mark with pins.
3 Divide ribbing into 4, with pins. Line up ribbing and neck edge pins (Fig iii).
4 Stitch neck seam with stretch seam (see Swimwear, Chapter 16).
5 Stitch other shoulder through ribbing (Fig iv).
6 Sew in sleeves whilst garment is flat, lining up shoulder points.
7 Sew on sleeve ribbing following neck instructions.
8 Join side seam and sleeve in one seam.
9 Finish hem with blind machine hem (Fig v).

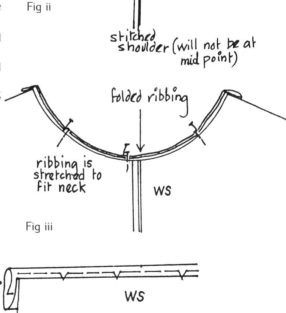

unstitched shoulder

WS

Fig ii

stitched shoulder (will not be at mid point)

folded ribbing

WS

ribbing is stretched to fit neck

WS

Fig iii

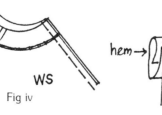

WS

Fig iv

hem →

WS

Fig v

Cross-over Fronts

Although most suitable for 'hour-glass' figures, this style looks well on any figure type.

When making the pattern we need a complete front block instead of the usual half block. The design in our diagram uses a yoke, onto which the front is softly gathered. The front waist darts are ignored and the waist area is also gathered to achieve a balance in design.

If designing a blouse only, the waist could be left straight to tuck into a skirt or trousers.

C
F

lengthen
for blouse

Fig i

1 Draw around one side of the front block to the waist line.
2 Turn block over, draw around the other side as Fig i, lining up centre-front lines.
3 Close shoulder darts in preparation for yoke.
4 Draw in desired yoke line (Fig ii). Mark notches where yoke is to join front. Cut away yoke.
5 Open out lower part of dart again (Fig iii). This becomes a gathered edge instead of using the dart (gathering line is 3.6cm (1½in) each side of dart lines).
6 Decide on a point on the CF line where top should cross *. Draw a broken line for cross-over, from 1.2cm (½in) into shoulder at neck, through * to waist line (can be any position in waist). (Fig iii)
7 Draw in facing, along dotted line 5cm (2in) from cross-over line.

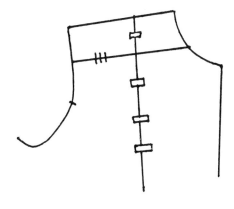

Fig ii

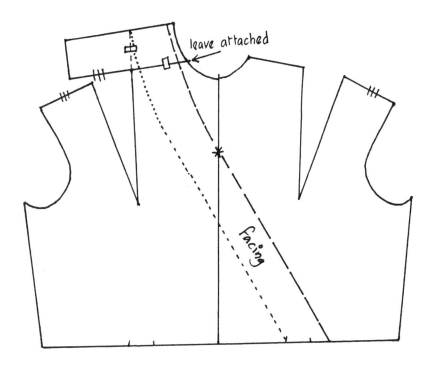

leave attached

facing

Fig iii

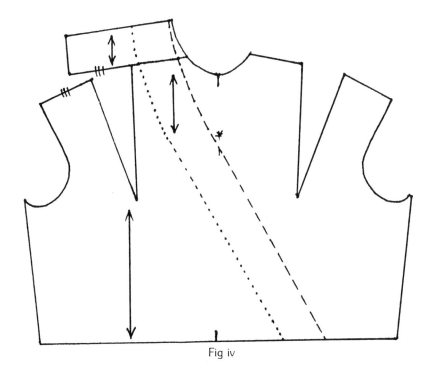

Fig iv

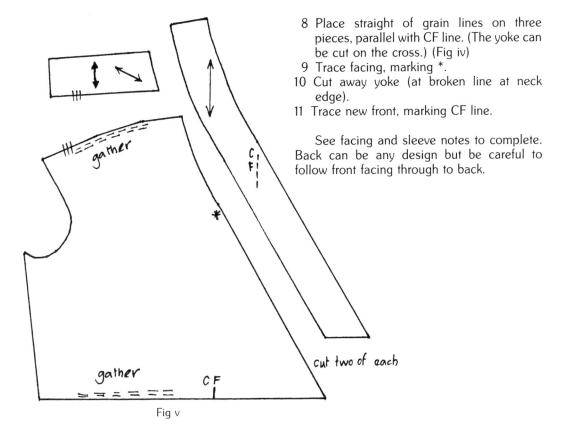

8 Place straight of grain lines on three
pieces, parallel with CF line. (The yoke can
be cut on the cross.) (Fig iv)
9 Trace facing, marking *.
10 Cut away yoke (at broken line at neck
edge).
11 Trace new front, marking CF line.

See facing and sleeve notes to complete.
Back can be any design but be careful to
follow front facing through to back.

gather

gather

C
F

*

cut two of each

CF

Fig v

13 Jackets

Basic Jacket Block

As jackets or coats fit over other clothes they need to be made larger. Apart from enlarging the bust/chest, waist and hip measurements it is necessary to make armholes and necklines deeper and to lengthen the basic blocks.

Collars and sleeves should be designed for the enlarged block although construction remains the same.

Back

1 Raise the neck edge on shoulder 0.6cm (¼in), to A (Fig i). Draw in a parallel line along shoulder, extending shoulder 0.6cm (¼in).
2 Curve a new line to centre back for neck, C.
3 Mark across back 0.6cm (¼in) wider to D. Lower underarm point 1.2cm (½in) to E. Connect new armhole points to form deeper curve.
4 At side seam, lower hip line 1.2cm (½in) to F. At centre back lower hip line 0.6cm (¼in) to G.
5 Connect G to F.
6 Draw in side seam, allowing 1.2cm (½in) right through.

On fitted jackets the centre-back seam is shaped to fit tighter at the waist. The back dart may also be increased for a tighter fit.

Depending on style, the back dart is sometimes made smaller, usually 1.2cm (½in), to increase waist size.

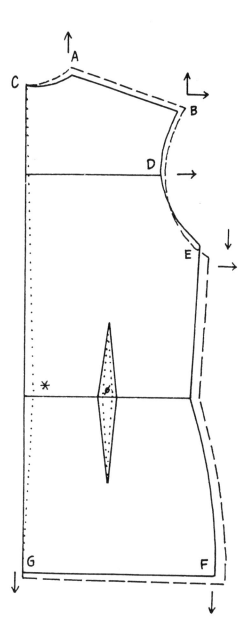

Fig i   Enlarged block (back)

Front

1 Raise the neck at shoulder 1.2cm (½in) and into shoulder 1.2cm (½in) to H (Fig ii).
2 Draw in new neck curve to original neck point (np).
3 Raise shoulder at armhole 0.6cm (¼in) and out 0.6cm (¼in) to match the back, at I.
4 Reduce shoulder dart, 1.2cm (½in) in all, by marking new points 0.6cm (¼in) each side of top dart, K. Make dart 2.4cm (1in) shorter and re-draw bottom of dart 0.6cm (¼in) towards centre front at J.
5 Raise both sides of darts at K 0.6cm (¼in).
6 Draw in new dart and shoulder lines.
7 Lower underarm point, L, 1.2cm (½in).
8 Widen across chest 0.6cm (¼in) to M.
9 Re-draw new armhole connecting these points.
10 Lower hip line 1.2cm (½in) at side seam, N.
11 Extend centre front 0.6cm (¼in) at O. Connect N to O.
12 Widen side seam 1.2cm (½in) right through.

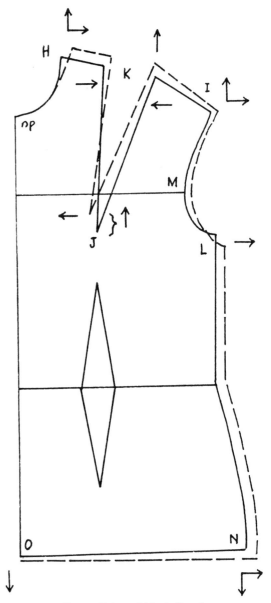

Fig ii   Enlarged block (front)

Jacket Sleeve

1 Widen the basic sleeve underarm seams 1.2cm (½in), the same measurement by which the front and back blocks were widened.

2 The sleeve head should be 2.4cm (1in) deeper to allow for new deeper armhole.

3 Follow example in Fig iii for shape but check measurement of total new armhole on front and back jacket blocks.

4 Measure new sleeve head. This should be 2.4–3.6cm (1–1½in) longer than armhole measurement.

If alterations are necessary, follow directions on altering the basic sleeve in Chapter 8.

Fig iii

Fig iv

Two-piece Sleeve

1 Make a fitted sleeve pattern from the basic jacket pattern (see Chapter 8).

2 In the sleeve head mark in points 5cm (2½in) at underarm.

3 On wrist line, mark in points 2.4cm (1in).

4 Connect points on front sleeve.

5 At elbow, measure amount in section *. Apply this measurement to back section at elbow, both sides of dart. Connect to underarm and wrist points.

6 Mark notches 15.2cm (6in) down from underarm and 15.2cm (6in) up from wrist.

7 Label and cut away sections.

79

8 Place two sections together, matching notches. The dart is closed out and the pieces become one unit (Fig v).

9 The remaining dart in the top-sleeve section is still to be sewn or can be gathered from about 5cm (2in) each side to fit back undersleeve (Fig vi).

10 If the jacket has front style lines going into the sleeve, the sleeve should be divided so that style lines meet *.

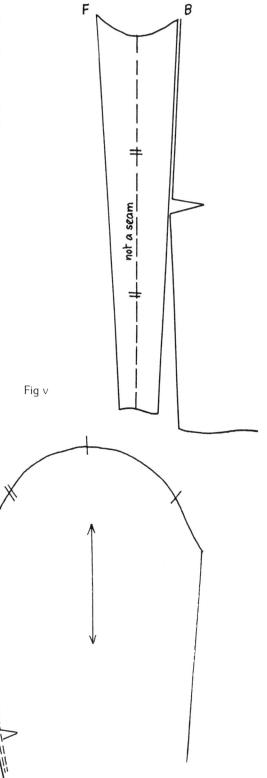

Fig v

Fig vi

14 Designing for men

Man's Block

The man's block is much less complicated than the women's due to lack of bust dart. The procedure for collars and sleeves is the same as the women's with plenty of choice.

The block in Fig i is for a 101.5cm (40in) chest, and can be used as a practice block. Fill in with individual measurements if desired. Measurements in square brackets in instructions are for the 101.5cm (40in) chest size.

You will need:

	cm	in
Chest	101.5	(40)
Back waist length	45.7	(18)
Front waist length	50.8	(20)
Shoulders	50.8	(20)
Across back	43.2	(17)
Across chest	45.7	(18)
Waist	86.5	(34)
Hip	101.5	(40)

Allow 10.2cm (4in) ease in the chest and hips.

Back

1 On the right side of paper, draw a vertical line to represent the centre back (Fig i).
2 AB = 25.4cm (10in), for hip to waist levels. Draw lines across paper.
3 BC = 45.7cm (18in), for back waist length. Draw line half way across paper.
4 Neck = chest with ease, divided by twelve. [111.7÷12 = 9.3cm (44÷12 = 3¾in)]. Apply this measurement from C to D. Mark a point 1.2cm (½in) above D. Draw in curved neck line.
5 Divide shoulder measurement in half [25.4cm (10in)]. Mark a point this measurement to E. From E measure down 3.2cm (1¼in) to F. Connect F to D to form the shoulder line.
6 From C measure down 22.9cm (9in) to chest line, G. This measurement will vary

with individual height.
7 From G measure across one quarter of the chest measurement with ease to K. [28cm (11in)]
8 CH = 15.2cm (6in). Apply half the across back measure to J. [22.8cm (8½in)]
9 Draw in armhole, connecting F, J and K.
10 AL = quarter hip measure with ease. [28cm (11in)]. Connect K to L.
11 On waist level on KL line mark in 2.4cm (1in) for waistline curve. Generally, the waist is not darted to a close fit but darts can be added for vests or fitted shirts. (Follow instructions for women's block.)

Front

1 On the left side of paper, draw a vertical line to represent the centre front.
2 MN = 25.4cm (10in).
3 Take chest line H (on back) across to W, chest line G to T and hip line A to M.
4 NO = front waist length. [50.8cm (20in)]. Draw broken line half-way across page.
5 OP = 9.3cm (3¾in). From O on centre-front line mark a point 9.3cm (3¾in) down. Join these points with a curved line for neck.
6 OQ = half the shoulder measurement. [25.4cm (10in)]
7 QR = 3.6cm (1½in). Connect R to P to form shoulder line.
8 On across-chest line apply half the across-chest measure to S. [22.9cm (9in)]
9 MV = quarter hip measure with ease. [28cm (11in)]
10 TU = quarter chest measure with ease. [28cm (11in)]
11 Connect R, S and U to form armhole curve.
12 UV is a straight line. Mark in 2.4cm (1in) at waist level, as back, and draw in side seam.

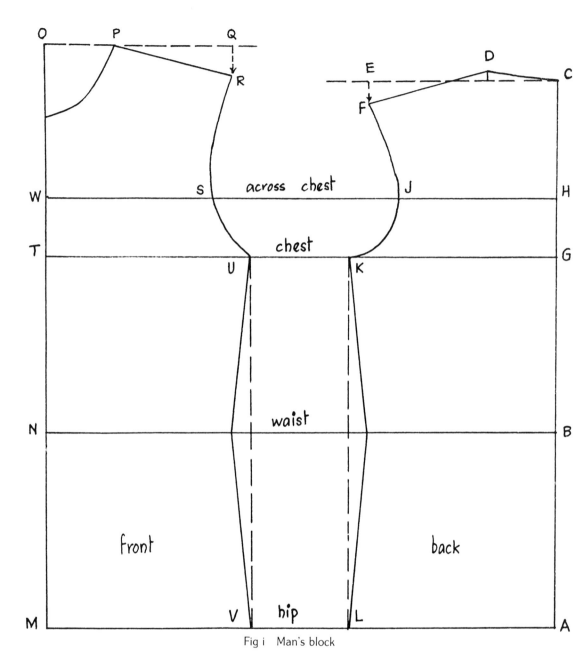

Fig i   Man's block

Men's Trousers

General Measurement Chart

	cm	in	cm	in	cm	in
Waist	94–99	(37–39)	76–91.5	(30–36)	71–75	(28–29½)
Front crotch length	26.7	(10½)	25.4	(10)	24.8	(9¾)
Back crotch length	29.2	(11½)	28	(11)	27.7	(10¾)
Hips	104+5	(41+2)	94+5	(37+2)	89+2.4	(35+1)
Outside leg	106.7	(42)	101.5	(40)	101.5	(40)
Hip level	22.9–24.1	(9–9½)	21.6	(8½)	20.3	(8)

Basic Trouser Block

1 Take individual measurements carefully (see notes on children's trousers, page 88).
2 Draw a rectangle, half the hip measure with ease × the outside leg measure.
3 Divide rectangle in half lengthways, F to G.
4 Draw in hipline, D to E.
5 Mark a point 2.4cm (1in), each side of F.
6 Draw in a curved line from these points to hipline, as Fig i, to represent sides.
7 Measure front waist. Take double front measure from actual waist measurement with any ease desired. This will leave the total back waist measurement. Divide in half.
8 Mark a point A from back side seam, at waist level, to the back waist measure plus 2.4cm (1in) for dart.
9 Mark another point midway between A and back side seam for dart position (see Fig i).
10 Mark 1.2cm (½in) each side of dart point. Draw down 10.2cm (4in) on central dart line. Connect points to form the dart triangle. (The dart can be eliminated for jeans or for styles with straighter back seam.)
11 To reduce the dart size and slope the back seam, draw a line to the CB line from bottom of dart (Fig ii). (See women's block also.)

12 Cut from CB to dart point and down left side dart line to point, leaving piece attached at point.
13 Slide piece to the right and lay the left dart line on to the central dart line. Secure in place.
14 The CB line is now raised and the dart is halved in size. Re-draw the back waist line with a slight curve.
15 Draw in front and back crotch lines.
16 Extend front 5cm (2in) and back 10.2cm (4in)
17 Draw in crotch curves from these points. The curved lines should lay approximately 1.2cm (½in) beyond hipline on CB and CF lines to allow more ease.
18 The hemline measurement will depend on style required but as a general rule mark a point 3.6cm (1½in) each side of G, and taper to these points from hipline to form the side seams.
19 Mark points 1.2cm (½in) each side of original rectangle, on hemline, and connect from extended crotch points to these, to form the in-seam lines.

As the crotch levels are different the hem may need to be straightened on the trousers. Care should be taken in sewing around the crotch, clipping the seams on curves.

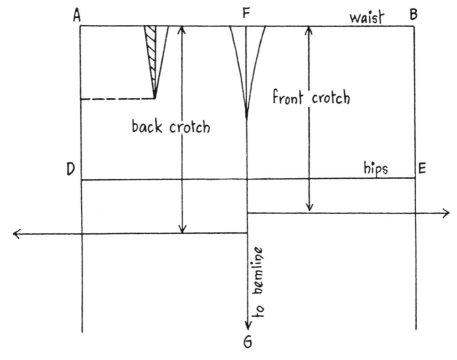

Fig i

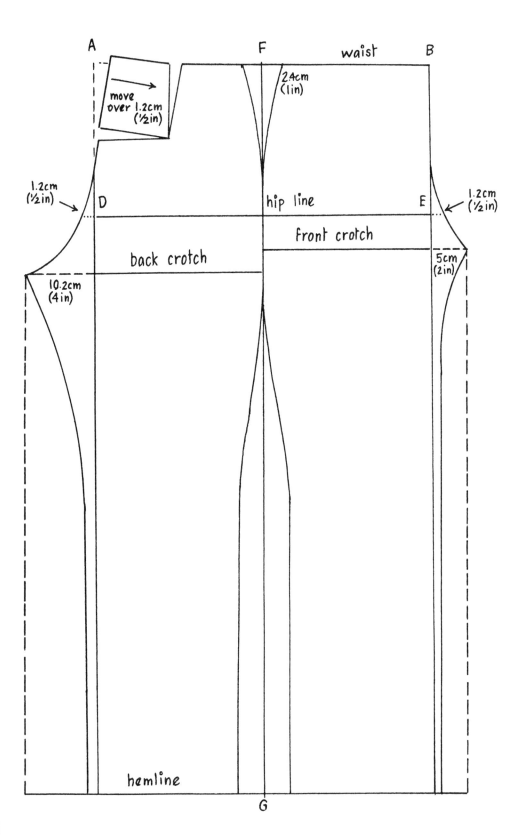

Shirt-type Collars

Men's shirt styles have changed very little over the last few decades. Shirt shoulders usually have a yoke. A variety of cuffs and collars can be achieved and the following styles are just as acceptable as women's styles with buttoning right over left.

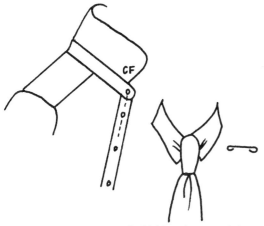

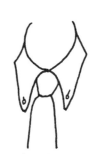

1 Long front button-down   2 Regular

3 Held under tie with bar through eyelet holes

4 Windsor – wider to allow for triangular knot

5 Small rounded

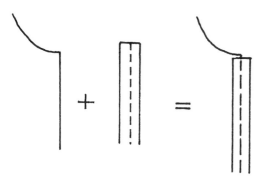

Fig i

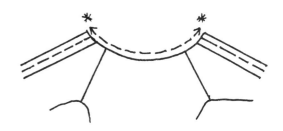

Fig ii

To construct a button stand to centre front add a band which should fit 1.2cm (½in) over centre-front line and 1.2cm (½in) back (Fig i). The band will be cut double in fabric.

To make a neck band, first measure the neck, including the band, * – * (Fig ii). Draw a straight band approximately 2.4cm (1in) wide × neck measurement (Fig iii). With a view to collar being worn with a tie, design collar to sit 'back' from centre front. Collar edge that fits band is straight, but outer edge can vary.

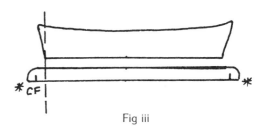

Fig iii

15   Children's patterns

Basic Child's Block

The child's block is simple since it does not require shoulder or waist darting. Darts can be added to the waist on older children for more fitting styles. Often younger children have a larger waist than chest measurement. As 3.6cm (1½in) is added into this block for ease, consideration must be taken with the initial lay-out to accommodate a large waist measure. Fig i shows an easy method of adding to the waist, especially since the extra is only necessary in the front *.

The following basic measurements (given in centimetres, with inches in brackets) are taken from commercial patterns and may be helpful if the child is not available for fitting, or, for making clothes commercially. A column is provided for you to enter your required measurements.

Approx age	2		4		6		8		10		12		Name
Chest	53.3	(21)	58.4	(23)	62.2	(24½)	66	(26)	71	(28)	76	(30)	....
Waist	50.8	(20)	53.3	(21)	56	(22)	58.4	(23)	61	(24)	63.5	(25)	....
Hips	50.8	(20)	63.5	(25)	66	(26)	71	(28)	76	(30)	82.5	(32½)	....
Back waist length	22.9	(9)	24	(9½)	26.7	(10½)	29.2	(11½)	31.8	(12½)	33	(13)	....
Dress length	45.7	(18)	52	(20½)	62.2	(24½)	72.4	(28½)	72.4	(28½)	73.7	(29)	....
Sleeve length	26.7	(10½)	35.5	(14)	40.7	(16)	40.7	(16)	40.7	(16)	42	(16½)	....
Around arm	19	(7½)	20.3	(8)	21.6	(8½)	22.9	(9)	24	(9½)	28	(11)	....
Crown depth (sleeves)	8.3	(3¼)	8.3	(3¼)	8.9	(3½)	8.9	(3½)	10.2	(4)	11.4	(4½)	....
Across chest													....
Across back													....

NB The measurements given in square brackets throughout the following instructions for the basic block are for a child age 6.

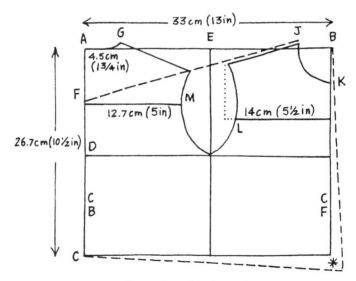

Fig i   Basic block age 6

1 At top of paper, draw a horizontal line AB = half chest measurement with ease. [62.2+3.6 = 65.8. 65.8÷2 = 32.9 (24½+1½ = 26. 26÷2 = 13)]
2 Draw a vertical line from A to C = back waist length. [26.7 (10½)]
3 Complete the rectangle.
4 Draw a horizontal line midway between AC, called D; draw across rectangle for armhole level. [13.3 (5¼)]
5 Draw a vertical line midway between AB, called E, as block division. [16.5 (6½)]
6 F is midway between AD. Raise F 0.6cm (¼in).
7 On F, draw a line horizontally to a point half the across-back measure to M. [12.6 (5)]
8 AG = the neck width, approximately one third of the across-back measurement. [4.2 (1¾)]
9 From B, on the centre-front line, apply the same measurement to J and down to K. Raise G and J 1.2cm (½in).
10 Join G to A and J to K with curved lines for necklines.
11 On centre-front line, mark a point midway between K and armhole level. Draw across horizontally, the across-chest measure to L. [14 (5½)]
12 From L, mark a point 1.2cm (½in) to left. Draw a vertical line from this point touching FJ line (broken line on Fig i) to become the shoulder point. (See dotted line on Fig i.)
13 Measure the front shoulder line. [10.2cm (4in)]. Draw back shoulder line from G to same measurement. Place rule at the 10.2cm (4in) mark on G, angle rule until it touches the F to J line. The shoulder lines will not be at the same angle and will be adjusted on the toile, following instructions for the women's block to centralise this line.
14 Draw in complete armhole, connecting shoulder points at armhole level through M and L.

The underarm seam sometimes needs to be moved back about 1.2cm (½in) as many children are wider in the front than the back. This too will be adjusted from observation at the toile fitting.

All collars and sleeves can be constructed for the child's block following instructions for the women's garments.

For children with rounder stomachs, extra shaping can be added to the front. (See Fig i, broken line *.)

Basic Sleeve

1 Draw a rectangle, the around-arm measurement × the sleeve length. [21.6×40.7 (8½×16)]
2 Divide lengthways into four sections.
3 Mark lines for back (B), top (T) and front (F) positions, following Fig ii.
4 From B, mark a point down 3.2cm (1¼in).
5 From F, mark a point down 3.6cm (1½in).
6 From top line, measure down the crown depth. [8.9 (3½)]
7 Draw in sleeve head curve as Fig ii.

It is not usually necessary to curve the wrist line.

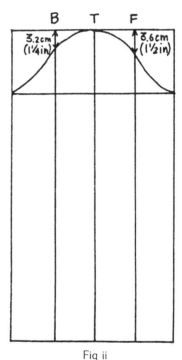

Fig ii

Child's Trousers, Pyjamas and Underwear

Measurements required for this block are:

Waist ....

Hips ....

Crotch length ....

Outside leg length ....

Bottom leg width ....

Underwear

NB Measurements in square brackets are for a child aged 6.

1 Draw a horizontal line, half the hip measurement with no ease, at waist level AB. [33cm (13in)]

2 Draw down the crotch length, AC. [24.1cm (9½in)]

3 Form a rectangle with these four points.

4 Draw a vertical line through the centre of the rectangle for side seam. Measure from waist the desired depth to top of leg at X (Fig i). [17.8cm (7in)] This measurement should be taken individually.

5 On CD line measure 3.6cm (1½in) in from left to a point, F and 3.6cm (12in) in from right to a point G. Draw leg arch through F, X and G.

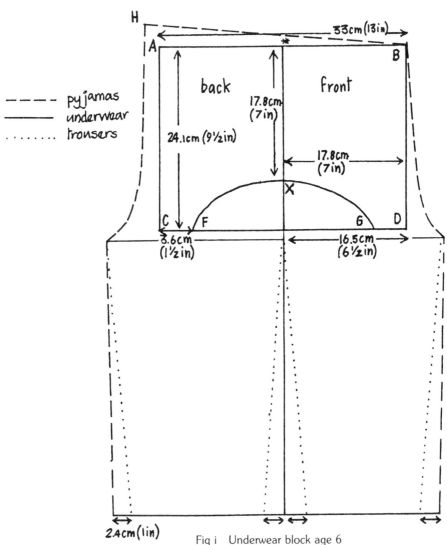

Fig i   Underwear block age 6

Extending the underwear block for pyjamas and trousers

1 Extend A upwards 2.4cm (1in), and to the left 2.4cm (1in) to H (Fig i).
2 Draw in new waist line curving from H to B. At centre point *, the new line will be approximately 1.2cm (½in) above the original AB line.
3 Drop CD line 1.2cm (½in).
4 Mark a point to form the curved crotch lines, 7.6cm (3in) to left of new C, and 5cm (2in) to right of new D.
5 Connect H to this extended back point with a curved line and B to the front point (Fig i).
6 From waist level draw down the outside leg measure for pyjamas or wide trousers. This style is very popular designed with an elastic waistline. Extend the waistline up twice the elastic width plus seam allowance.

To taper legs of this style, divide difference of total hem measure and desired hem measure by four. Deduct equally from inside and outside leg seam lines (see Fig i).

Corrections that may be necessary
Look at the child's total side view and imagine a central line through waist and hip into the leg. This is where the side seam in a garment should 'sit'. If a child's stomach is extra rounded, or he/she has an exceptionally hollow back, the line will pull towards the part needing extra fabric in the garment.

To add extra for the stomach, first measure from the side seam line towards furthest position of stomach, imagining a line dropped to * (Fig ii). Check the crotch extension measure on the block. (Point D was extended 5cm (2in).) If more width is needed, possibly extending to the new measurement will correct this problem.

Check the crotch curved line from midway between legs to waist, on child. An easy method of achieving this is to join the zero ends of two tape measures together. Place joined point under body as centrally as possible, and bring tapes to front and back waist individually (Fig iii). The child may need to hold the tape under him/her.

Make a note of new measurements and measure block for any difference.

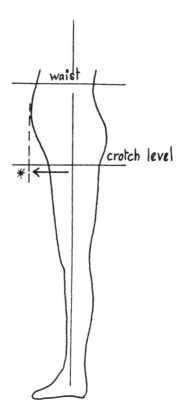

Fig ii

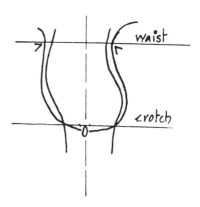

Fig iii   Measuring for crotch curve

To further lengthen front for stomach
The previous measurements will determine the amount of any further lengthening of the front seam.

1 Draw around the front block.
2 Cut across to the side seam halfway between waist and crotch lines (Fig iv).
3 Open out CF line to required measure, thus leaving side seam as it is.
4 Re-draw CF and side lines.

To lengthen back
The measurements taken earlier will also determine whether extra length is necessary in the back. Follow the same method as lengthening the front.

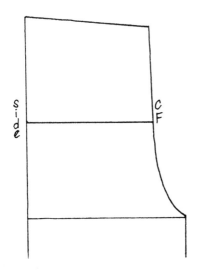
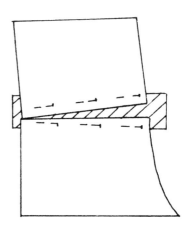

Fig iv

16 Lingerie

Since underwear fits closer to the body and is usually made in stretch fabrics you will need to take off most of the ease allowance on the basic blocks. The normal basic block allows 5cm (2in) in the bust, 2.4cm (1in) in the waist and 7.6cm (3in) in the hips.

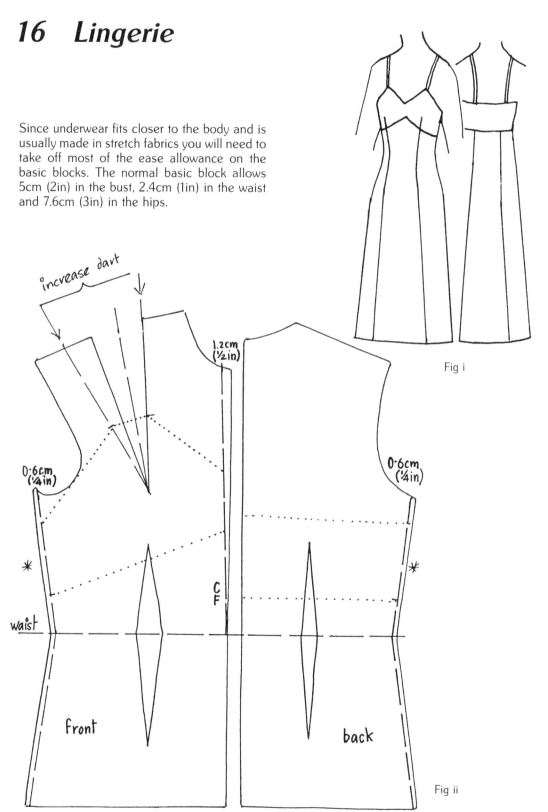

Fig i

increase dart

1.2cm (½in)

0.6cm (¼in)

0.6cm (¼in)

C F

waist

front

back

Fig ii

Slip

The basic slip (Fig i) has a bodice with a lower bust dart and princess-style body. Straps are usually 0.6cm (¼in) wide ribbon.

To Prepare the Basic Block

1 Draw around the basic F and B blocks (Chapter 4).

2 Remove 0.6cm (¼in) from front and back sides.

3 Mark a point 1.2cm (½in) in on CF neck (Fig ii). Taper a line from this point to existing waist on CF. Remove piece.

4 Increase the shoulder dart. Take out extra towards shoulder line or equally each side of shoulder dart.

5 Draw in bodice shape for slip in Fig i. (See dotted line, Fig ii.) Make each side of dart from bust point, level, as dart is to be closed out.

Sides should start 2.4–3.6cm (1–1½in) lower than original block to allow freedom of movement. Bodice sides must be equal *–*.

6 Cut away bodice sections, marking grain lines.

7 Draw a line directly under end of shoulder dart to top of waist dart (Fig iii(a)). Close out shoulder dart (Fig iii(b)). Cut up to bust point, thus enlarging waist dart to accommodate bust fullness.

8 On the back bodice, continue centre dart line to top (Fig iv). Draw in new dart lines by connecting top point to each side of dart at bottom (Fig iv(a)).

9 Close out dart (Fig iv(b)).

Mark notches where dart was closed as these will line up with back princess seam.

Straps should be sewn to original dart positions and length required can be measured from initial diagrams.

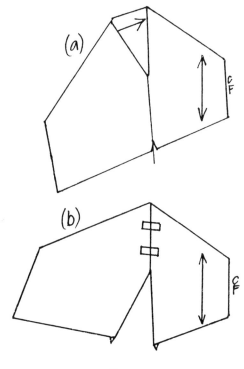

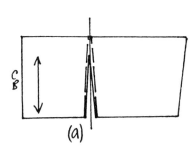

Fig iii

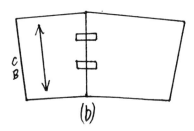

Fig iv

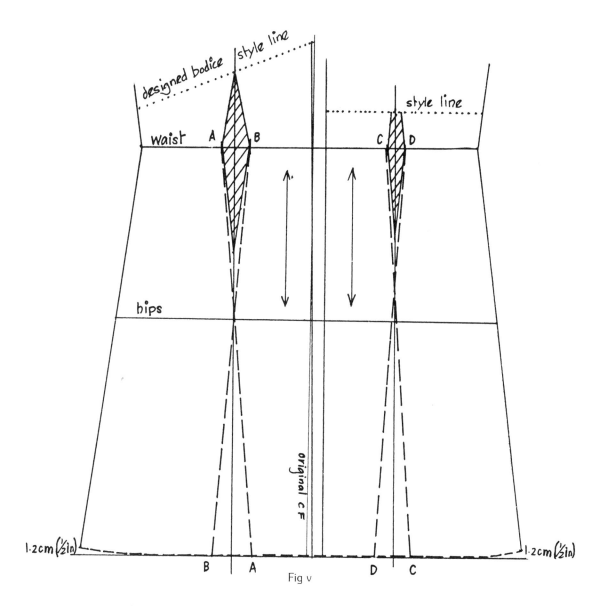

Fig v

Lower Section

1 Draw around the lower front and back blocks with reduction. Continue to required hem. Hem should be 2.4–3.6cm (1–1½in) shorter than dress length. Shaded area shows original dart.

2 Draw vertical lines through centre of darts to hem (Fig v).

3 At hem mark a point 2.4cm (1in) each side of lines. Connect these points to each side of darts at waist, A to A and B to B. By not following the original dart lines when designing this pattern a closer fit is produced.

4 Raise side lines at hem 1.2cm (½in). Draw in curved hemline.

5 Mark with notches and trace each section separately. Grain lines should run parallel with CF and CB lines.

93

Alternative Top to Slip

A slip bodice can be designed in several ways, styles depending on the shoulder dart. The following design uses the dart to form gathers on the CF line.

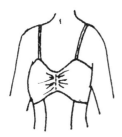

1 Draw around the bodice section of basic slip block.
2 Connect each side of the waist dart to bust point with dotted line (Fig i).
3 Close the waist dart on the dotted line (Fig ii).
4 Open out the shoulder dart to incorporate the waist dart, thus making it larger and re-draw the lower edge line, connecting to CF (Fig ii).
5 From BP draw a horizontal line to CF line (Fig iii). Measure centre-front line and make a note of this.
6 Close the shoulder dart (Fig iv). Cut along horizontal line to open fullness to CF. The front should be gathered to original measurement.

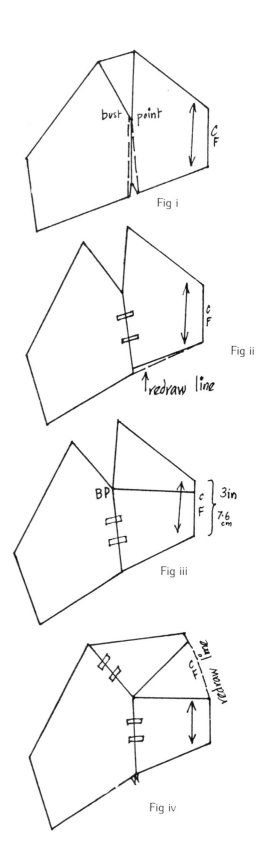

Fig i

Fig ii

Fig iii

Fig iv

Panties/Bikini Bottoms

You will need to construct this block separately. Reduce actual body measurement by 5–7.6cm (2–3in) if constructing panties in stretch fabrics. For woven fabrics use actual hip measurement without ease. The example above is for a 91.5cm (36in) hip size.

1 Draw a rectangle 28cm (11in) deep × half the hip measurement. AB = waist level.
2 Mark a point, C, halfway between AB. Draw a vertical line down to D.
3 EF = hip level. Use individual measurement from skirt or trouser block, minus 1.2cm (½in). (The 20.2cm (8in) becomes 19cm (7½in).)
4 From E, the centre-back line, measure across 14cm (5½in).
5 From F, the centre-front line, measure across 11.3cm (4½in).
6 Drop centre-back line 2.4cm (1in) to G.
7 Drop centre-front line 1.2cm (½in) to H.
8 Mark across the crotch width from these points, 6.3cm (2½in). Mark a point 3.6cm (1½in) above hip line on CD line. This is a fairly high leg pantie but this can be adjusted to suit the individual.
9 Draw in curved leg lines as in Fig i. The back is wider and is usually strengthened with elastic on construction.
10 Design crotch liner lines (Fig ii). Add notches. These pieces should be traced and joined together as pattern pieces and can then be sewn as one unit. (See notes on construction of underwear and sewing swimwear, etc in Chapter 17.)

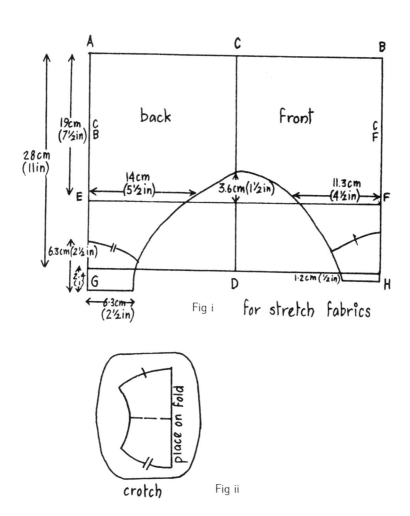

Fig i for stretch fabrics

crotch Fig ii

95

Bra/Bikini Tops

From the basic slip block we can make a
separate block for bra or bikini tops. These
garments should be made in elastic or two-way
stretch fabrics and further reduction of the slip
block is necessary.

The shoulder dart has already been enlarged
and any further size reduction can be made by
darts at the initial fitting (Fig i**).

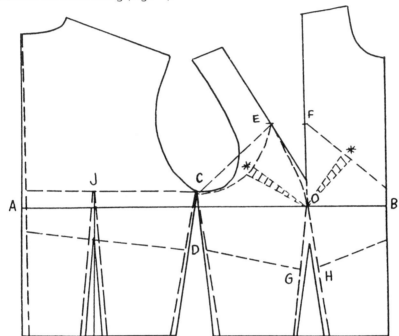

Fig i
——— = slip block
– – – = bra block

1 Draw around the slip blocks to waistline,
   touching at sides.
2 Extend the right side of the shoulder dart
   2.4cm (1in). Draw a horizontal line through
   this point, O, from centre back to centre
   front, A to B.
3 At centre back, mark points 2.4cm (1in)
   above A and 3.6cm (1½in) below. This can
   be adjusted to suit individual design and
   need.
4 At side seams on front and back, mark
   points 2.4cm (1in) above AB line to C, and
   5cm (2in) below to D.

5 On front, mark points 10cm (4in) above O,
   on shoulder dart, E and F. Mark points
   7.6cm (3in) below O, on waist dart, G and
   H.
6 Draw a horizontal line across back from C
   to centre back.

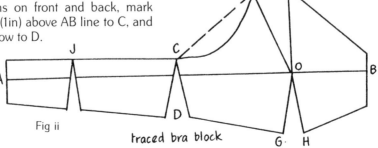

Fig ii

traced bra block

joined as one unit

Fig iii

7   Draw a central line through back waist dart to J.
8   Mark points 1.2cm (½in) each side of waist darts, each side of side seams and at centre back. Connect front dart points to O, back dart points to J, and centre back point to neck.
9   Draw a line from D to centre back to form lower edge of back bra.
10 On centre front line, mark points 2.4cm (1in) above and 5cm (2in) below B. Join upper point to F and lower point to H.
11 Join C to E with either a curved or straight line. A curved line will be most comfortable.
12 Join E to O with a slightly curved line.
    When all pieces are joined together (Fig iii), the joining points can be rounded off.

Basic Bra

1   Follow steps in Fig i.
2   Trace bra block (Fig ii).
3   Join dart and side seams (Fig iii).

Horizontal-seamed Bra

1   To make this style, first follow steps on basic bra (Fig i). Trace bra block (Fig ii). Join dart and side seams (Fig iii).
2   Close front vertical darts. Open out horizontally, from side seam to centre front along AB line (Fig iv).
3   Separate pieces to form a seam line.
    This bra is usually made up with elasticated fabric such as Spandex at back and plain knitted fabric, usually nylon or polyester, on front.

Gathered-front Bra

This softer styling makes the gathered front bra popular for exercise and sleep bras.

1   Draw around the bra front in Fig iv.
2   Close the horizontal dart in the side section to open the front out wider (Fig v). The centre front should be gathered to the measurement of the basic bra in Fig i.

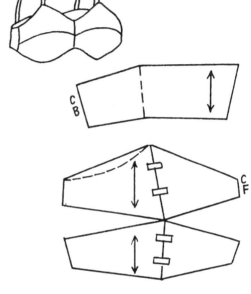

Fig iv

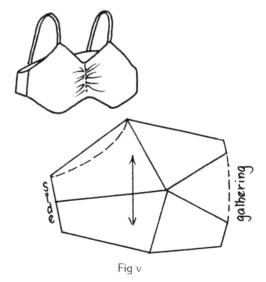

Fig v

One-piece Swimsuit

1 Trace around the bra block to the waistline. Include style lines for bra, if to be used, and darts.
2 Trace pantie back block connecting waist to top back.
3 The front will need to be placed separately. Draw section at CF to desired style line on leg (X). This will be the division line for the front panel. Mark point of division X on pattern being traced.
4 Trace side front to X. Connect each side of waist dart to X points.

5 On back, draw central line through dart and waist to pantie leg *.
6 Connect sides of dart to *. This may be used as the division lines for back panel or as a shaped dart.
    If unsure of fit, since this further reduces the pattern, make up as dart as they can be adjusted.
7 Measure for straps. Allow extra for crossing at back.

Swimsuits retain their shape better if lined. Use a swimwear knit lining. To reinforce legs stitch seam with slightly stretched swimwear elastic.

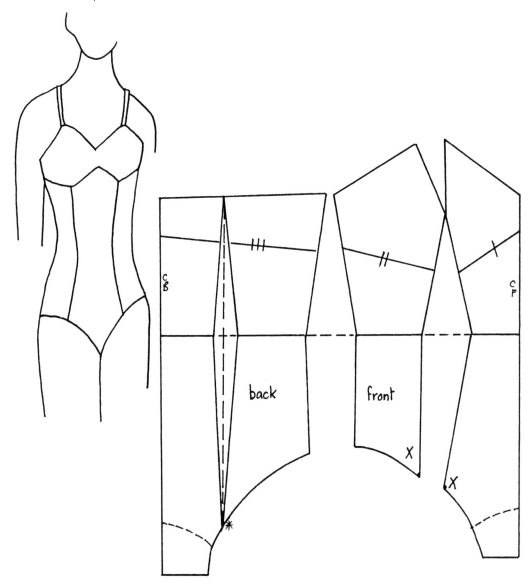

17   Fabrics

Before purchasing fabric for your new designs the following list of certain properties may be helpful. It is a good idea to check with the sales assistant if unsure of a fabric.

Natural Fibres

Cotton Very absorbent, soft, smooth and cool to wear. Strength increases when wet. Blends well with other fibres. Can be processed or finished, eg mercerized for lustre. Pre-shrink before construction.

Linen Good heat conductor, absorbent and strong. Often bleached before selling. Blends well with other fibres. Can be treated for crease resistancy, water repellancy, stain, spot or mildew resist. Pre-shrink before construction unless treated.

Wool Good insulator and absorbent. Creases. Can be felted or shrunk. Dry clean unless blended with another fibre. Can be treated for wash and wear and with 'Scotchguard' for stain resistancy. Sew tip: Clean before, use silk thread, fine needle and short stitch.

Silk Lustrous, durable and resilient. Warm in winter; cool in summer. Dry clean only unless blended and labelled otherwise. Sew tip: Use only silk thread, fine needle and medium stitch length. Loosen tension for shantung. Sew over tissue paper on sheer or glossy silks.

Man-made Fibres

Nylon Extremely strong. Will not shrink. Resists moth and mildew. Low absorbency so can be warm to wear, however knitted types help overcome this. Helanca is added for swimwear stretch. Does not tear easily. (Nylon is made from coal.)

Polyester Resistant to creasing, chemicals, weathering, mildew and moths. Low absorbency. Blends well with other fibres. Finishes include anti-stat. (Polyester is made from petroleum.)

Triacetate Similar to acetate but more robust.

Resistant to creasing, soiling, shrinking and stretching. Low absorbancy. Can be knitted into fine jersey. Often used for quilts and hand knitting yarn.

Acetate Rich appearance. Good draping qualities. Resilient and moth proof. Easy to dry and shrink resistant. Blends well with silk, cotton, wool, rayon and nylon. Frays; allow extra yardage. Sew tip: use synthetic thread. Press with tissue paper under seams to prevent line showing on outside.

Rayon Can be straight, crimped, bright or dull. Anti-stat properties so is the most popular blending fibre. Absorbent and retains whiteness. Blends well with natural fibres also. Can be treated for wash and wear, water repellancy, spot, stain and mildew resistancy. Sews like cotton. Pre-shrink before use.

Acrylic Bulky fibre but soft and warm. Lightweight, non-irritant. Resists fading moths, mildew and chemicals. Frays; allow extra.

Sewing with Furs

Fake furs can be made of acetate, acrylic or rayon. They usually have a knitted or woven backing and should be dry-cleaned unless otherwise stated.

Design
Use simple styles – fabric becomes the main feature.
Silhouette is affected by shagginess of fur.
Eliminate details such as pocket flaps and tailored collars unless using smooth- or short-hair furs. Use 'grown-on' facings, ie not joined by a seam.
Raglan or dolman sleeves are easier to wear.
Trim fur with leather or vinyl as a feature. Fur itself is sometimes used as a trim on yokes, sleeves, cuffs.
Fastenings should be simple: toggles, hooks, snappers.

Cutting
Cut pile fabrics in a downwards direction only.

A toile of the pattern made up previously is the best way to judge fit. Any alteration can then be made to the pattern before cutting in fur.
Place pattern on wrong side of fabric. Cut one piece at a time. Very shaggy piles need to be cut with a razor thus only cutting backing and not fur (real fur is cut this way).
Add ample seam allowance.
Cut under-collars in smooth fabric, knit or woven, but must match fur type. Cut smaller so seam will roll to underside of collar.
Interfacings should be chosen to match main fabric, knitted or woven.
Real fur should be mounted onto a closely woven fabric before sewing.

Sewing

Stitch with loose tension: stitch length 8–10 stitches per 2.4cm (1in), medium needle.
Decrease foot pressure when sewing several layers. Always test on scraps first.
Machine in direction of pile.
Pull pile that gets caught in machining through on right side with a pin. Brush.
Any darts should be cut through centrally and left flat. Neaten by overlocking.

Pressing

Steam can be used but often finger pressing is sufficient. Usually fur garments do not require a tailored look.
Short hair types can be treated as velvet: use sleeve board or towelling on an ironing board. Work on wrong side with iron held about 1.2cm (½in) above fabric, not actually making contact but forming steam.

Swimwear or Two-way Stretch Garments

Design

Design from the reduced swimwear block.
Pre-shrink fabric, lining and elastic. Use swimwear elastic.
Before laying pattern out, determine direction of stretch. Stretch usually goes around the body.

Cutting

Place pattern pieces on wrong side of fabric. Using ball-point pins, pin within seam allowances.
Label pattern pieces on wrong side with tape if pieces are small or unusual shape. Lining should be cut identical to main garment and sewn together as one piece. (This is called mounting.)

Sewing

Use synthetic thread, fine machine needle – ball-point or designed for knits. Contrary to general belief it is not necessary to own a machine with special stitches for sewing swimwear or any other knits.

Straight-stitching machines
Using a medium-length stitch, stretch fabric as you sew.
Sew seams twice.
Hand finish to overcast edge or stitch another row of straight machining 0.3cm (⅛in) from seam.
Trim to 0.6cm (¼in).
Sew elastic with two rows, one at each edge.

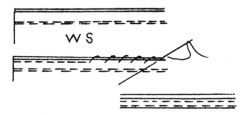

Zig-zag machines
Sew seams and any top-stitching with a medium-length stitch on narrowest zig-zag.
Trim seams to 0.6cm (¼in).
Overcast with wider zig-zag.
Use large open zig-zag to attach elastic.

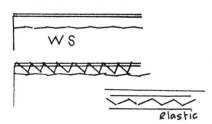

Reverse-cycle machines
Sew with stitch that overlocks as it seams.
Use elastic straight stitch for top-stitching.
For elastic use three-step zig-zag.

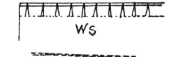

Elastic

Elastic is used within the seam to give a snug fit around neckline and leg openings. Measure, with elastic stretched to a comfortable fit, around the body.

Seam allowance on these edges should be basted to the wrong side. Lay elastic over raw edge and stitch in, stretching to fit.

See notes on elastic waistbands (page 125) and measuring for stretch bands on T-shirts (page 73) to ensure proper fitting.

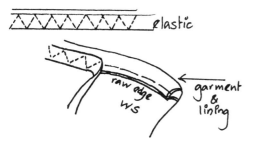

See-through and Lace Fabrics

Design

No pockets.

Buttonholes should be machine- or hand-sewn. Button loops look neater.

Eliminate darts where possible; design with minimum amount of seams.

Using coloured fabric behind sheer enhances effect.

Care needed where solid fabrics join sheer. Solid should be of similar properties in weight and stretch/ease.

Cutting

Cut in single layers.

Thread-mark any points that must be noted, ie darts.

Use sharp scissors and smooth cutting surface. Use fine needles rather than pins and pin within seam allowance.

Leave extra turnings on fraying fabrics.

Position lace and prints: centralise designs.

Sewing

Use fine needle: stitch length 15–20 stitches per 2.4cm (1in) for sheers; 8–10 stitches per 2.4cm (1in) for lace.

Seams: use french or narrow overlocked (see Figs i–iv).

Any bindings can be made on the cross from same fabric (Fig v).

If using lining fabric sew darts as one unit as in mounting (Fig vi).

Cut dart open and neaten edges.

Seams can be sewn through tissue paper.

Pressing

Cool iron for sheers.
Medium heat for laces.
NO steam.

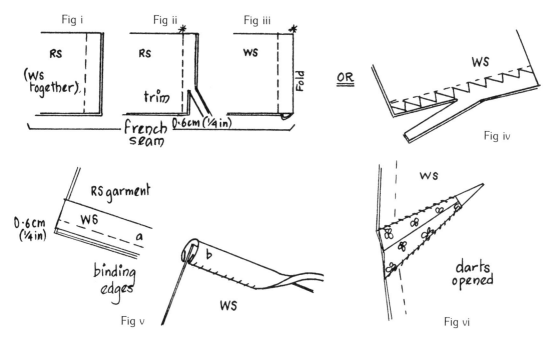

Vinyls and Wet-look Fabrics

Vinyl, polyurethane and Cire are all transparent film-covered fabrics.

Design

Use simple designs, avoiding curved seams.
Sleeves are easier to work with if raglan or loose style.
Top-stitching holds turnings flat.
Patch pockets work best; avoid tailored types.
Make a feature of fastenings; zips are fairly easy to put in.

Cutting

Make sure garment fits well. Previously making a toile of pattern is advisable, then alterations can be made to pattern before cutting in vinyl.
Pin only within seam allowances or tape pattern to fabric.
Darts and markings can be made using a chinagraph pencil.
Cut with paper on surface to avoid sticking.

Sewing

Use a medium needle for woven fabrics with medium stitch length.
If possible fit machine with a roller foot.
Use buttonhole thread for top-stitching.
Welt seams are stronger but flat seams work well.
Facings can be made in a matching non-vinyl fabric.
Layer all seams.
Interfacings are not normally necessary. Using muslin behind buttonholes or at the back of pocket top adds strength.
Waistbands can be made in grosgrain ribbon for comfort; Vinyl does stick to the skin.

Pressing

Finger press or rub handle of scissors along wrong side of seams.

Mock Bound Buttonholes

1 Carefully cut out rectangle for buttonhole in garment and any facing that will cover it (Fig i).
2 Fold 2.4cm (1in) strips in half for each side of buttonhole – longer than opening (Fig ii).
3 Sandwich between garment and facing. Top-stitch around rectangle (Fig iii).

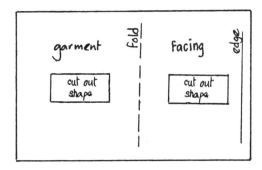

Fig i

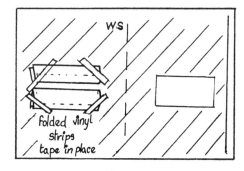

Fig ii

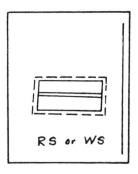

Fig iii

Underwear

As well as your pattern designed from the reduced lingerie block you will need:

Fabric Usually nylon is manufactured in 2.7m (108in) widths so purchase the garment length only.

Needles Fine ball-point or needles designed for knits.

Needle lube A liquid that is applied to the top machine thread to eliminate static which causes most synthetic thread to snap.

Elastic Fluted lingerie type for legs. Flat lace type for pantie or half-slip waistband.

Thread Polyester – good brand name.

Before cutting

Find the correct side of nylon fabric stretch along edge, about 25cm (10in). The fabric will roll to the right side.

Allow only 0.6cm (¼in) seam allowances.

When making straps, woven fabrics should be cut on the bias and knits on the straight grain. Sew seams as instructions for swimwear on page 100.

Making Panties with Crotch Seams enclosed within Crotch

1 Attach crotch from same fabric to F and B garment pieces (Fig i).
2 Sew cotton liner to one side of crotch seam. Garment piece is now sandwiched between (Fig ii).
3 Attach other side of liner to other side by sandwiching this also between (Fig iii).
4 Turn through – seams are enclosed. Finish side seams, legs and waistband (Fig iv).

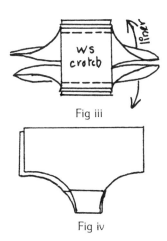

Fig iii

Fig iv

Working with Stripes, Checks and Patterns

Designing your own patterns can be advantageous when working with patterned fabrics. You will probably have a general idea of the design you will be working with. Shop for your fabric first as style lines, etc can be altered to suit the fabric. Allow extra yardage.

For example: A skirt for a 96.5cm (38in) hip person could be cut from approximately 115cm (1¼yd) of 115cm (44in) fabric without nap (nap refers to pattern in this case).

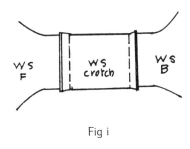

Fig i

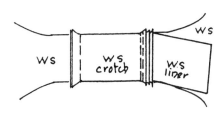

Fig ii

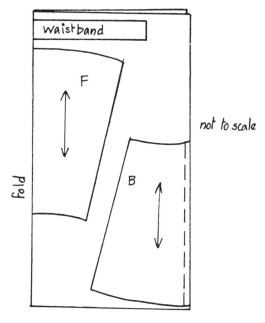

Fig i   Fabric without nap

103

Use the layout in Fig ii if using an uneven check and use the skirt length approximately twice [1.6m (1yd)]. This could also be a

There are two types of design, even or uneven. This applies to checks, floral or striped fabrics.

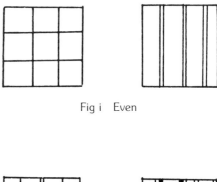

Fig i   Even

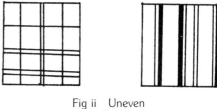

Fig ii   Uneven

An even fabric can be prepared for cutting by folding on required line and pinning design upon design. Cut pattern piece as normal for two equal but opposite sides.

If your fabric is a natural fibre such as wool, silk or cotton have it cleaned and blocked before beginning. For cottons that will be laundered pre-washing and ironing is sufficient.

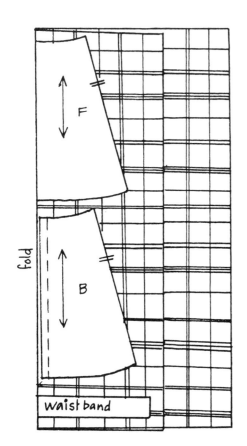

Fig ii   Fabric with nap

flowered fabric with the flowers all facing one direction. Care is needed when positioning large flowers.

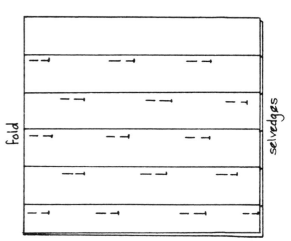

With an uneven pattern decide whether the pattern is to go around the garment or contrast.

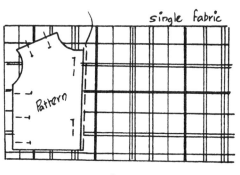

single fabric

Pattern

Fig iii

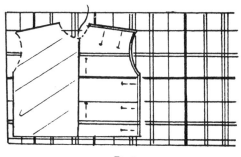

Fig iv

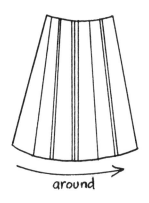

around

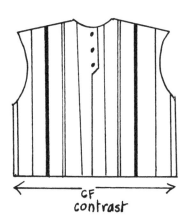

CF
contrast

To cut an uneven fabric with pattern in opposite directions
1 Trace pattern piece as it is easier to work with left and right pieces.
2 Position right side at an acceptable place on single fabric.
3 Turn left side over and position to matching points.

It is sometimes helpful to mark certain points with coloured markers for easier matching, ie the double line entering the neck on the diagram*.

NB The design must be printed through the fabric for this layout.

To cut an uneven fabric in one direction
1 Pin one side of pattern down at desired point (Fig iii).
2 Baste line along central line. There will not be a seam.
3 Cut around piece to baste line but not along it.
4 Remove pattern.
5 Fold cut fabric piece on basted line to form opposite side (Fig iv).
6 Pin well, matching pattern.
7 Cut second side.

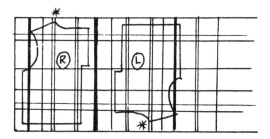

To cut a chevron effect

Unless pattern is evenly flared at CF, CB and side seams the fabric pattern may not line up at all seams.

It is usually more important to match CF and CB seams.

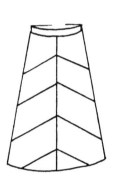 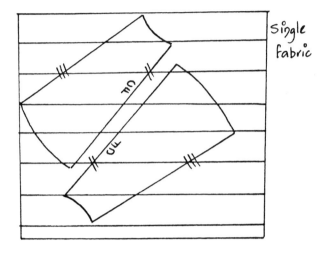

Single fabric

18 Sewing know-how

Bound Buttonholes

1 Mark position of buttonholes. Length should be width of button plus 0.3cm (⅛in). If a row of buttonholes is to be made baste on the machine starting and finishing lines. Buttonholes can be marked with a tracing wheel on tracing paper (Fig i).

2 Reinforce backs with interfacing. Iron-on interfacings work well but should be of correct weight for fabric. Stretch fabrics need stretch interfacing.

3 Cut oblong patches in main fabric, each measuring 5cm (2in) wide and about 2.4–3.6cm (1–1½in) longer than the required buttonhole. Pin patches over marked buttonhole positions, RS to RS (Fig ii). Baste through centre of buttonhole line.

4 Machine-stitch the rectangle, sewing the sides 0.3cm (⅛in) away from central line (Fig iii). See that the number of stitches on ends correspond. Overlap the last few stitches and fasten off ends. Remove basting.

5 Cut through centre of rectangle to within 0.6cm (¼in) of each end. Cut diagonally into the corners with care (Fig iv).

6 Turn patch through the slot to WS, pulling out corners carefully, so that you make a smooth rectangle. Press flat (Fig v).

7 Pleat each side inwardly to the slot, so that two folded edges meet in the centre and fill the rectangle like two parallel rows of piping (Fig vi).

8 Turn to RS and backstitch through these folds with small stitches (Fig vii). On WS folded ends will look like inverted pleats. Secure each end with a few stitches. Trim away any unnecessary patch fabric. Press (Fig viii).

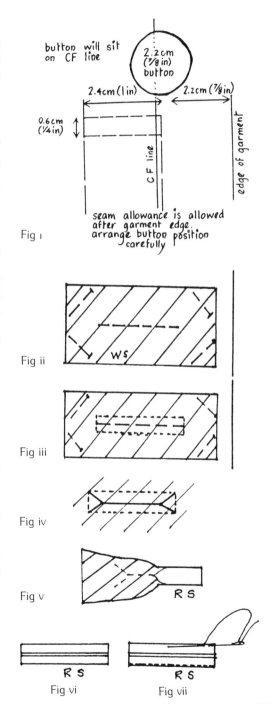

Fig i

Fig ii

Fig iii

Fig iv

Fig v

Fig vi   Fig vii

When front is to be faced the facing must have buttonhole slots corresponding to buttonholes. Lining fabric can be used to decrease bulk. Follow steps 1–6. Machine top-stitch around rectangle (Fig ix).

Slipstitch, by hand, both sides together (Fig x).

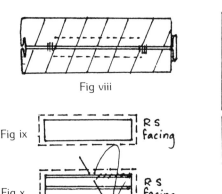

Fig viii

Fig ix

R S facing

Fig x

R S facing

Hand-worked Buttonholes

An alternative to machine buttonholes, these are cut first. Make sure lengths and positions are marked exactly.

1 Using a buttonhole twist thread make a few 'running' stitches to start. Work in whichever direction is comfortable to you. Bring the needle from the back through at required stitch length, 0.3cm (⅛in), on front (Fig i). Hold the thread from the end nearest the eye and take it around the needle point. Pull the needle through to form a chain stitch on buttonhole edge. Continue along one side.
2 Form a half circle at this end with whipping stitch. Use an uneven number of stitches, preferably 7 (Fig ii).
3 Using buttonhole stitch complete the other side. Work 4 whipping stitches at the end, the width of both sides (Fig iii).
4 Work 7 blanket stitches across these 4 stitches to neaten end. Blanket stitch is worked from left to right. Start with thread * (Fig iv), take needle under stitches with point through at desired width. Put thread under needle and pull through.
5 Finish with a few stitches, over and over, on wrong side.

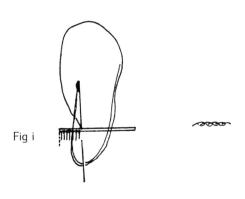

Fig i

Fig ii

7 stiches

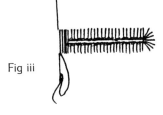

Fig iii

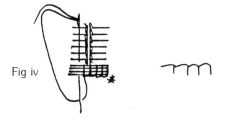

Fig iv

Machine-made Buttonholes

1 Setting the machine will vary on different models. Check your instruction manual; usually the needle should be in the LEFT position (Fig i).
2 Stitch length almost to 'O' (Fig ii); varies with fabric.
3 Stitch width at medium (Fig iii), then widest.

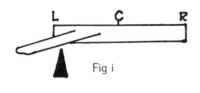

Fig i

Fig ii

Fig iii

Preparation
Prepare your garment with two rows of basting stitching, one where the buttonhole is to start and the other at the end.

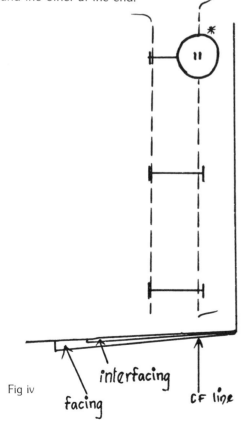

Fig iv

interfacing

facing

CF line

The buttonhole should be the button size plus 0.3cm (⅛in). Measure the space between each buttonhole and mark each position, with chalk or tailor's tacks.

NB On fronts (dresses, blouses, etc) the buttonhole should end 3cm (⅛in) over CF line. The corresponding button will be sewn on the CF line * (Fig iv).

Sewing
1 Zig-zag down the left side of the buttonhole. End with the needle on the right but still in the fabric.

2 Lift foot, turn fabric so the stitching is now on the right. Lower foot and take one stitch, moving machine by hand. Leave needle out of fabric.

3 Alter the stitch width to wide. Make about 5 stitches to form end bar. Take needle out again.

4 Put stitch width back to medium and continue stitching to form other side. Stop just before end.

5 With needle out of fabric, change stitch width to wide and make other end bar (approx 5 stitches). Adjust machine to straight stitching. Reverse to make a few finishing stitches.
6 Cut through centre with unpicker or sharp embroidery scissors.

Continuous Strip Opening
(sleeves)

When a sleeve is to be fitted at the wrist, either by cuff or otherwise, a neat opening must be made to allow for one's hand to go through. This method is simple and can be used on any fabric type.

1 Decide the length of opening, usually 6.3cm (2½in). This should be made on the 'B' line of the sleeve (see page 30). Cut a straight line, not tapering (Fig i).

   The binding strip should be twice the length of the opening by 2.4cm (1in) and cut on the cross (bias) (Fig ii).

2 Reinforce both the strip and sleeve edges. For the sleeve start 0.6cm (¼in) in on lower edge and taper to the top of the opening, allowing enough to stitch only (Fig iii).

   The strip should be reinforced with a continual 0.6cm (¼in) line (Fig iv).

3 Place the strip to opening, RS to RS (Fig v). The midway point of the strip * (Fig iv) should touch the top of the opening 'O'. Make a 0.6cm (¼in) seam with a small machine stitch.

4 Turn under 0.6cm (¼in) on other edge of strip. Fold over to bind edge and hand-stitch in position on WS (Fig vi).

The binding should be folded under on top cuff that has buttonhole and remain flat on under-cuff that holds button (Fig vii).

   This opening can also be used at front-neck openings where buttonholes are not required. A loop and button are usually recommended at the top on neck point.

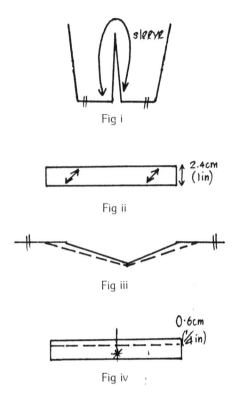

Fig i

Fig ii

Fig iii

Fig iv

Fig v

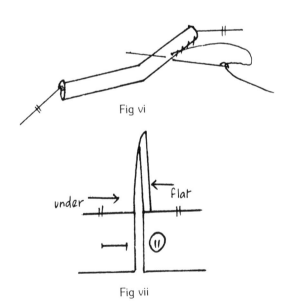

Fig vi

Fig vii

Curved Hems

1 Mark hem from floor, with rule, to desired
length. Wear shoes that are to be worn with
garment. Cut away surplus fabric allowing
3.6cm (1½in) for hem below pinned hemline (Fig i).

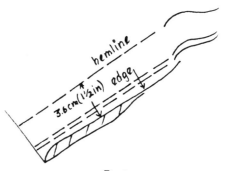

Fig ii

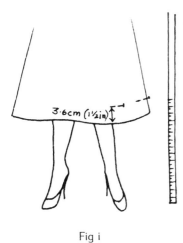

Fig i

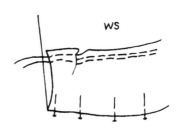

Fig iii

2 With largest machine stitch, make a single
line around finished hem position, leaving
thread ends as these will be removed later.
Make two rows of machining at hem edge,
again leaving ends and using large stitch
(Fig ii).
3 Pin up from hem line using single row of
machining as a guide. Press. By pulling
double row of stitching threads, ease surplus
fabric at edge to fit garment (Fig iii).
4 Finish edge by stitching with herringbone
stitch or apply bias tape, fold up and blind-
stitch hem into position (Fig iv).

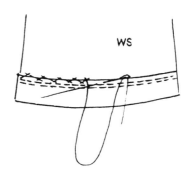

Fig iv

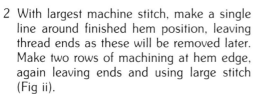

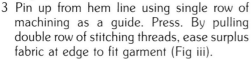

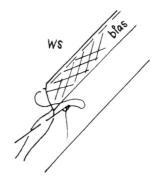

Fly-front Zip

1 Stitch front seam with regular stitch length to fly bottom, around under seam, to * (Fig i). Baste remaining fly seam with largest machine stitch. Leave thread ends for easy removal later. Clip to * and press basted part of seam open.

2 Baste waist seam 1.6cm (⅝in) from garment top as guide to placing zip (Fig ii). Most zip manufacturers allow 1.8cm (¾in) from zip head to top of tape. This allows room of 0.2cm (⅛in) between seam line. If zip head were to be placed directly below the 1.6cm (⅝in) seam it would appear bulky and pull fabric.

3 With open zip face down, pin right side of zip to right fly flap. Teeth should sit on basted seam. Stitch through tape centre, on fly flap only; not through garment (Fig iii).

The machine needle should be on the left of zip foot to allow stitching closer to teeth.

4 Fold back closed zip so that right side is facing you. (About 0.3cm (⅛in) will show beyond the normal seam line.) With needle on right side of zip foot, stitch along this 0.3cm (⅛in), close to zip teeth (Fig iv).

Press zip and fly flat.

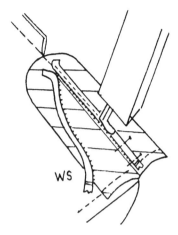

Fig iii

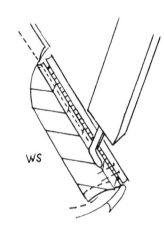

Fig iv

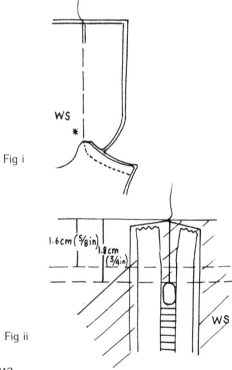

Fig i

Fig ii

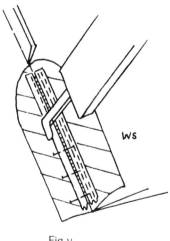

Fig v

112

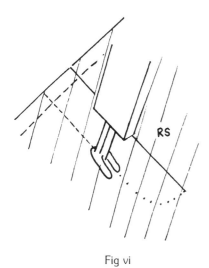

Fig vi

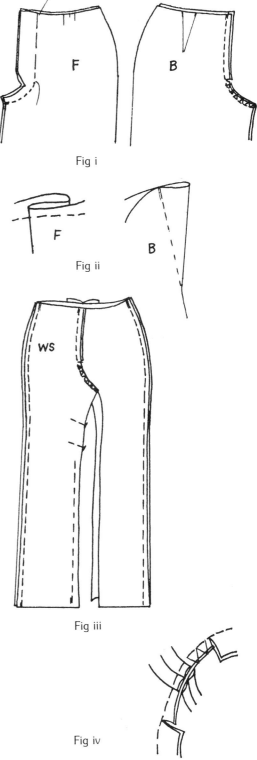

Fig i

Fig ii

Fig iii

Fig iv

5 Change zip foot to allow needle on right of foot. Holding already stitched side clear, pin left side of zip into position through fly only (Fig v). Stitch through centre of tape. Press again.

6 On right side of garment, mark desired fly curve line. Bottom should end 0.6cm (¼in) beyond zip end.

Fly is usually 3.6cm (1½in) wide. Make sure fly flap will be caught in the seam line on wrong side. Line is usually 3.2cm (1¼in) from centre.

7 Using regular machine foot, stitch fly curve line (Fig vi). Remove basting.

Zip 'sits' back about 0.3cm (⅛in) so is completely concealed.

Reverse left – right directions for man's fly-front zip.

Making Up Trousers

1 Stitch back curved seam. Reduce to 0.6cm (¼in) at curve and overlock seam (Fig i). Stitch front to end of zip position. Strengthen curve as back.

Follow instructions for fly-front zip (page 112) if to be included in design.

2 Stitch front pleats and back darts (Fig ii).

3 Sew outside and under-leg seams RS to RS (Fig iii).

4 Reduce seam under crotch to 0.6cm (¼in) and overlock for strength (Fig iv).

5 Interface waistband, trimming to 0.6cm (¼in) from edges thus layering seams (Fig v). Press up one side, leaving a 1.6cm (⅝in) seam allowance.

Fig v

6 Pin waistband into position RS to RS with unpressed edge to trouser edge (Fig vi). The overlap should be on the left side for women's trousers and on the right side for men's.

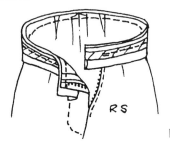

Fig vi

7 Fold back ends of waistband and stitch a 1.6cm (⅝in) seam (Fig vii). Trim away corners and turn to right side and press. Pressed edge is now ready for hemming and saves judging the fold (Fig viii).

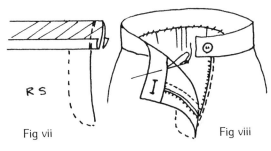

Fig vii   Fig viii

8 Attach hook and bar fastener or make button and buttonhole closure.
9 Press in front and back creases if desired.
10 Hem trouser bottoms to required length (Fig ix).

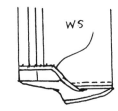

Fig ix

Flap Pocket

1 Decide on the pattern of the flap. Cut 2 with turnings and 1 in interfacing. Interface one side. With RS to RS stitch around outside edge (Fig i). Turn through and press well. Top-stitch if desired at this stage.

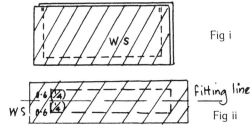

Fig i

Fig ii

2 Cut piece of interfacing to strengthen back of pocket at least 2.4cm (1in) longer than finished pocket length. Secure to WS garment behind pocket position (Fig ii). Mark pocket position on both sides of garment.

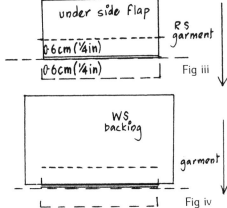

Fig iii

Fig iv

3 Place flap with raw edges on position line, with RS of flap to RS of garment. Baste into position, or stitch (Fig iii).
4 For pocket back, cut a piece of lining 3.6cm (1½in) longer than finished pocket in width and the required pocket length (approx 12.7cm (5in)). Place RS down centrally on same line as flap (Fig iv).
  Machine-stitch through flap and lining to the exact pocket size.
5 Place a piece of self-fabric, same size as previous lining, RS down on fitting line on opposite side. The edges of flap and lining should touch this piece (Fig v).

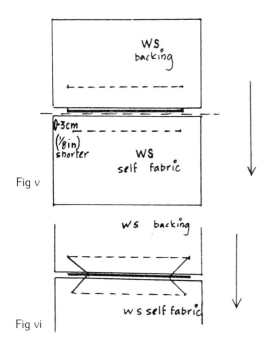

Fig v

Fig vi

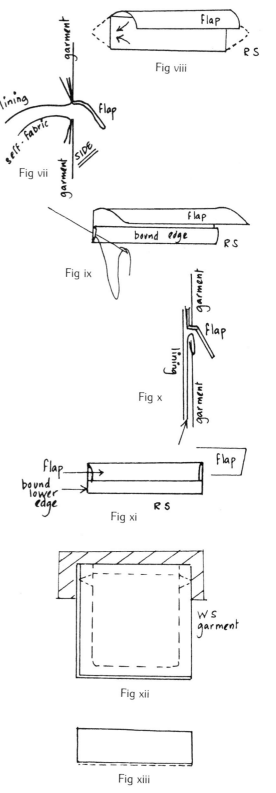

Fig viii

Fig vii

Fig ix

Fig x

Fig xi

Fig xii

Fig xiii

6 Machine-stitch into position but slightly shorter than flap line. This will allow for folding through and ensure flap will fit *over* opening.

7 Cut along fitting line to within 1.2cm (½in) of ends. Cut out to corners (Fig vi).

8 Push lining and backing through opening to WS (Fig vii shows a side view). The triangular ends should be pressed away from opening.

9 The pocket opening can be left as a rectangular opening as the flap will cover it (Fig viii).

or

Ease the self fabric up to form a bound edge appearance before it falls down to be joined to lining (Fig ix). It will be necessary to hand-stitch sides of bound edge into position and for strength. Fig x shows a side view. The flap can then be tucked in as an alternative feature (Fig xi). A better fit is achieved if the flap is designed with a slanted edge on the side to tuck in more easily.

10 On WS stitch around pocket, curving corners at bottom (not through garment). Be sure to 'catch' triangular pieces at sides within stitching (Fix xii).

The top of pocket line can be stitched down also (Fig xiii).

Patch Pockets

1 Mark position of pocket on garment (Fig i).
2 Cut out pocket to desired style, adding seam allowances of 1.2cm (½in) around and 3.6cm (1½in) at top.
3 Cut interfacing to exact pocket size with no seam allowances (Fig ii).
4 Cut lining to pocket size with seam allowance around but not the 3.6cm (1½in) at top (Fig iii).
5 Place interfacing to WS of pocket fabric. Use padding stitch for attaching non-iron-on types (Fig ii).
6 At top of pocket, turn over 3.6cm (1½in) hem to outside on RS. Stitch through ends with 1.2cm (1½in) seam. Clip corners. Turn to WS. Press well and press seam allowance around pocket in position (Fig iv).

or

Place pocket to lining, RS to RS. Stitch around sides. Leave top open. Clip corners. Turn through and press (Fig v).
7 Hand-stitch top pocket hem to lining (Fig vi).
8 Position pocket onto garment. Strengthen top corners of pocket with interfacing pieces on WS of garment (Fig vii).
9 Top-stitch pocket to garment using triangular shapes at the top for strength, catching interfacing pieces (Fig vii).

If making two pockets be sure to construct all processes together thus eliminating any risk of pockets not matching.

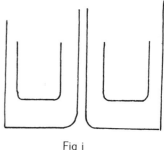

Fig i

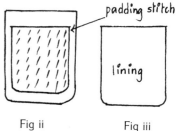

Fig ii   Fig iii

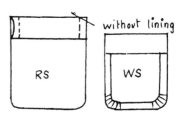

Fig iv

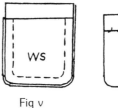

Fig v   Fig vi

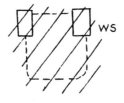

Fig vii

Fig viii

Welt Pocket

Most suitable for smaller top pockets.

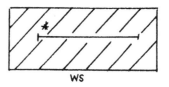

Fig i

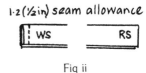

1·2 (½in) seam allowance

Fig ii

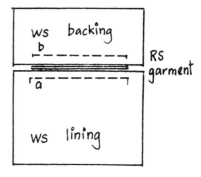

Fig iii

Fig iv

1 Mark position of welt on garment. A row of stitching is best * (Fig i).
2 On wrong side of garment, attach a piece of interfacing the pocket length + 2.4cm (1in) and 5cm (2in) wide. Any grain line on the interfacing should match the garment grain direction. Iron-on interfacings save time; choose one transparent enough to see position stitching.
3 Make welt of double fabric, interfaced, the desired length × approximately 2.4cm (1in) wide when finished. Make a 1.2cm (½in) seam each end with welt folded right sides in (Fig ii). Turn through to right side and press.
4 With folded edge of welt toward lower edge of garment (hem), baste welt into position. Raw edges should touch stitched position line * (Fig iii).
5 Take a piece of garment material, 3.6cm (1½in) wider than welt across, therefore overlapping 1.8cm (¾in) each end. Piece should be 7.6cm (3in) deep (Fig iii). Place right side to right side of garment touching position line from other side.
6 Machine both pieces down with 0.9cm (⅜in) seam. The stitching on the backing at (b) should end 0.3cm (⅛in) shorter than welt stitching (Fig iv).
7 Baste a piece of lining, same width as backing, but 17.8cm (5in) deep, over welt line (a). Stitch again.
8 Join a piece of lining to backing, the backing width × 7.6cm (3in) (Fig v).

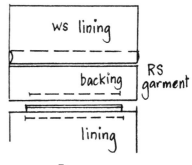

Fig v

117

9 Cut between stitching to within 0.6cm (¼in) of each end (Fig vi). Cut into corners.
10 Tuck backing through to wrong side. Press seam open. Tuck triangle ends to wrong side and pin back (Fig vii).
11 Fold front lining through also and press welt up (Fig viii).
12 Sew a 1.2cm (½in) seam to join pocket pieces, enclosing the end triangles in the stitching (Fig ix). Stitch pocket free of garment.
13 On right side blind-stitch welt into upright position (Fig x).

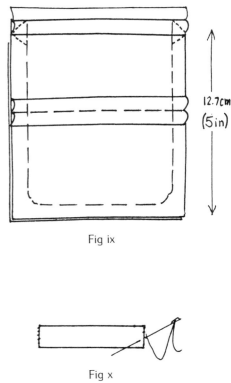

Fig ix

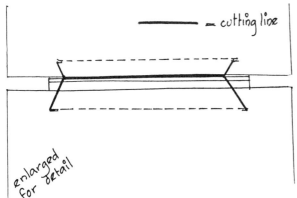

Fig vi

Fig x

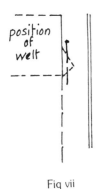

Fig vii

Fig viii

Attaching a Shirt-type Collar

1 Interface undercollar. Cut 0.6cm (¼in) smaller. Interfacing is shaded. Press seam allowance on neck edge to WS (Fig i).
2 With RS to RS stitch outside collar seam. Trim seams in layers (Fig ii). Cut corners away to allow for a sharp point.
3 Turn through to RS. Pull out corners with a pin if necessary. Press well. Only the top collar neck seam should be visible (Fig iii).
4 Stay-stitch neck edge of garment 1.2cm (½in) in from edge. Clip at 1.2cm (½in) intervals to stitching, but not through (Fig iv).
5 Turn back facing RS to RS. Stitch to CF line only (Fig v). Facing should be stay-stitched and clipped at garment neck edge (Fig vi).
6 Turn through. Neck seam allowance stands up.

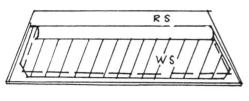

Fig i

7 Place RS of top collar to WS of garment at neck edge. Stitch seam from CF to CF holding folded edge of undercollar clear (Fig vii).
8 Cut out 'V's along seam and press seam into collar.
9 Hem undercollar down (Fig viii). Hand-stitch facing at shoulder position.

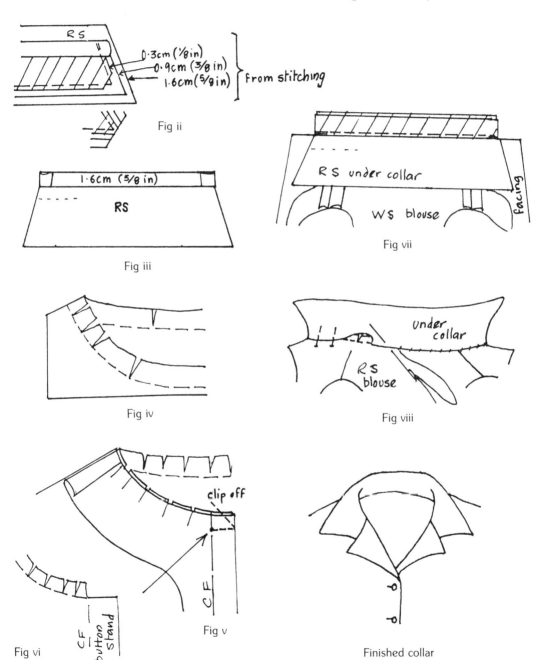

0.3cm (⅛in)
0.9cm (⅜in)
1.6cm (⅝in) } from stitching

Fig ii

1.6cm (⅝ in)
RS

Fig iii

RS under collar

WS blouse

facing

Fig vii

Fig iv

under collar

RS blouse

Fig viii

clip off

CF

Fig v

CF
button stand

Fig vi

Finished collar

Attaching rever complete with back collar

1 Add seam allowances to your pattern throughout. Cut all pieces in fabric.
2 Join fronts to back at shoulders, extending into neck seam allowance * (Fig i).
3 Join centre-back seam of undercollar RS to RS (Fig ii).
4 Interface top collar/facing pieces.
5 Join top collar pieces at centre back RS to RS (Fig iii).
6 Press all seams open.
7 Stay stitch the curved neckline seam lines and clip at 1.2cm (½in) intervals, to stitching (Fig iv).
8 Join back neck seam.
9 Press seam up into collar (Fig v).

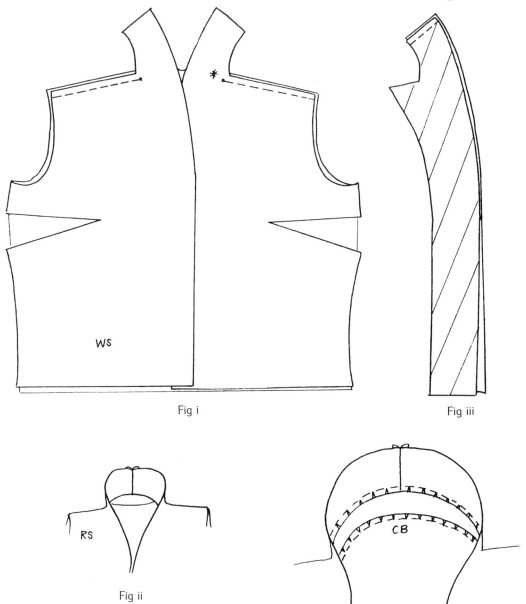

WS

Fig i

RS

Fig ii

Fig iii

CB

Fig vi

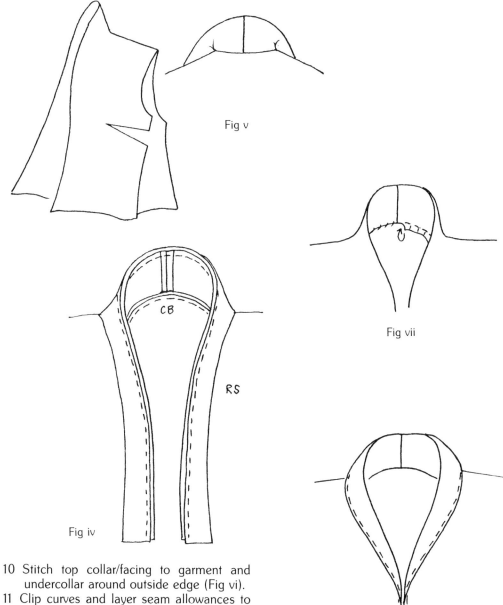

Fig v

Fig vii

CB

RS

Fig iv

10 Stitch top collar/facing to garment and undercollar around outside edge (Fig vi).
11 Clip curves and layer seam allowances to allow seam to lay flatter.
12 Press seam flat before turning facing to inside and pressing edge.
13 Neaten back neckline by turning seam allowance under and hand hemming (Fig vii).
14 Top stitching, if desired, is usually done after hemming.
15 Buttonholes should be worked next. See notes within this chapter on different types of buttonholes.

Shoulder Pads

Pattern

1 Place front and back blocks together on shoulder line (Fig i).
2 Draw around armhole to F and B notches. Mark shoulder line (Fig ii).
3 Measure depth of pad required on shoulder line, usually between 7.6–10.2cm (3–4in).
4 Connect from back notch to front notch in a good curve. Pad should overlap 0.6cm (¼in) into sleeve. (See broken line, Fig iii).
5 Trace broken line to become pattern, marking F and B points and shoulder line (Fig iv).

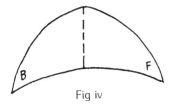

Fig iv

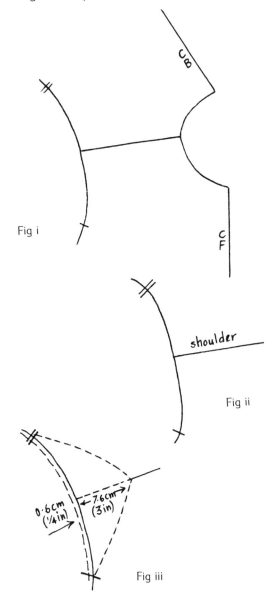

Fig i

Fig ii

Fig iii

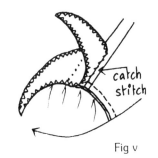

catch stitch

Fig v

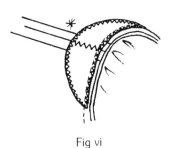

Fig vi

To Make Up

1 Cut four pieces of featherweight interfacing and two pieces of padding to pattern design. Padding thickness is of personal preference.
2 Sandwich padding between layers of interfacing. Stitch, using a large, open zig-zag machine stitch, all around edges. Straight-stitch along shoulder line.
3 Pad should be stitched into garment by sewing along shoulder seam allowance, thus making sure stitching does not show through on right side of garment.
4 Use loose catch stitch to secure at notches (Fig v).
   Alternatively, machine-stitch pad directly over sleeve seam.
5 Layer seams, ie pad is 0.6cm (¼in) from stitching, first seam should be 1cm (⅓in), second seam should be 1.2cm (½in) (Fig vi).

Tab Front

This type of opening has no front seam. It can be designed for any front but is mainly used on T-shirts for men or women.

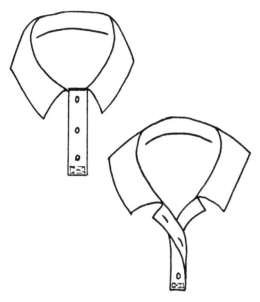

3 Design shirt-type collar measuring neck edge from * to * (Fig ii). (See Chapter 9 for shirt collars.)
4 Add seam allowances to garment and tabs. (1.2cm (½in) to edges; 1.2cm (½in) to joining edges; 2.4cm (1in) to lower tab.)

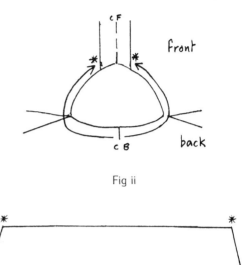

Fig ii

Pattern

1 Decide the length and width of tab. (The example here is 17.8cm (7in) long × 3.6cm (1½in) wide.)
   Tab is added to CF line with half width over CF line and half back into shirt (tabs overlap).
2 Mark positions of buttonholes. Allow for 1.2cm (½in) of stitching at bottom of tab (Fig i).

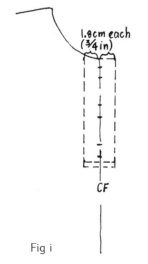

Fig i

To Make Up

1 Cut tabs double on fold. Cut two pieces in interfacing. Mark corners (X) where tab and garment front end (Fig iii).

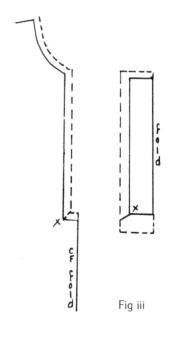

Fig iii

123

2 Sew in interfacing to one side of each tab. Fold back tab on fold line, RS to RS. Stitch across top with 1.2cm (½in) seam. Clip corners and turn to RS. Press well (Fig iv).

3 With RS to RS pin tabs to lengthways tab seam. Stitch both sides to X (Fig v). Clip diagonally to X points.

4 Press lower edge of opening to inside on seam line (Fig vi). Clip to corners.

5 Press tabs towards centre, left over right for men; right over left for women (Fig vii). Neaten inside seam edges.

6 Holding garment free of tab, pin lower edge of opening on garment to both overlapped tabs (Fig viii). Stitch across. Press. Neaten edges.

7 On RS strengthen lower tab with decorative stitching if desired (Fig ix).

8 Make lengthways buttonholes (Fig x) on right for women; left for men.

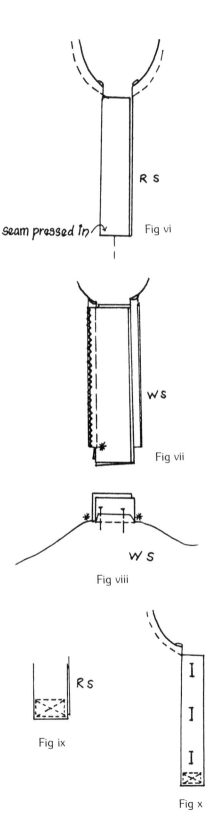

R S

seam pressed in

Fig vi

W S

Fig vii

W S

Fig viii

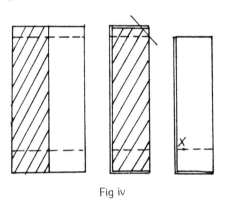

Fig iv

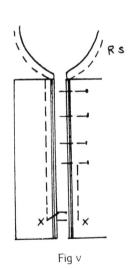

R S

Fig v

R S

Fig ix

Fig x

9 Neck edge can be neatened with a bias strip at this stage. Attach prepared collar with bias strip. (Strip = collar length + 2.4cm (1in) × 3.2cm (1¼in).) Sandwich collar between garment neck edge and strip, RS to RS, allowing 1.2cm (½in) each end of strip for turning under (Fig xi). Stitch.

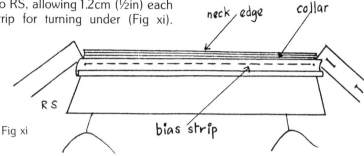

Fig xi

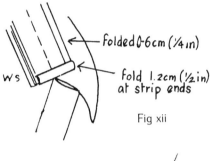

Fig xii

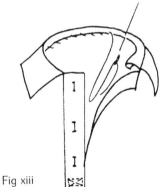

Fig xiii

10 Press 0.6cm (¼in) fold on other edge of strip (Fig xii). Trim seams to layered widths (see page 118).
11 Press strip to inside and hand-hem folded edge to garment (Fig xiii).

Tab fronts are often made up in different fabrics, complimenting the main garment. Sportswear shirts look and feel comfortable with the main body in a cotton knit and the tab and collar in woven cotton of another colour.

Elasticated Waistlines

Suggested Method for Trousers or Shirt with Sew-on Waistband

1 Make up garment leaving back inside seam of waistband open. Measure elastic around waist for a snug fit. Add 2.4cm (1in) for seam. Cut.
2 Secure a large safety pin or elastic threader to end of elastic and push through waistband. When 'tail' starts to disappear, pin down leaving approx 1.2cm (½in) out of seam. Continue to thread elastic out of opening. Remove pin.
3 Sew 1.2cm (½in) seam in elastic (Fig i). Close waistband opening and ease elastic evenly around waist.
4 At sides and back seam, stitch through to avoid elastic rolling (Fig ii).

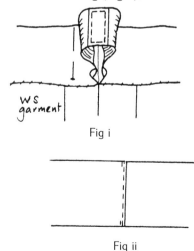

Fig i

Fig ii

For Waistlines without a Seam

NB To alter regular trouser or skirt pattern to this type of waistline, add the width of required elastic plus 0.6cm (¼in). Ignore any darting. Neaten top edge of garment.

1 Measure elastic as previous method. Make seam (Fig i).
2 Divide elastic band and waistline into quarters. Mark with pins.
3 Matching pins, place elastic into garment on wrong side so that the lower edge is on the casing foldline (Fig ii). (Casing foldline = width of elastic plus 0.6cm (¼in) down.)
4 Stitch, preferably with zig-zag, along bottom edge of elastic (Fig iii). The elastic should be stretched to fit garment. If you find it difficult to keep elastic straight, mark in line first with basting stitch or chalk.
5 Fold in to wrong side using the edge of the elastic as the fold line (to become the top edge). Stitching is now at top of inside edge only. Pin at regular intervals being careful not to twist 'band' (Fig iv).
6 Stretching elastic to fit garment, stitch through bottom of elastic with zig-zag (Fig v). This creates a waistband line on RS.

This method of adding elastic can be used to fit any edges together of different measurements in knits, eg neckbands or sleeve bands. Follow steps 1 and 2 to directly apply elastic to a waistline on any garment. For extra strength use the triple zig-zag machine stitch (Fig vi).

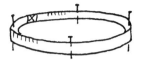

Fig i

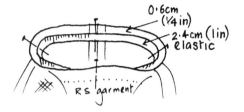

Fig ii

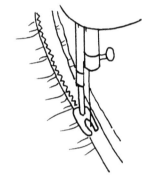

Fig iii

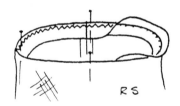

Fig iv

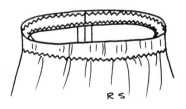

Fig v

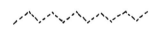

Fig vi

Index